HANNAH'S VOICE

HANNAH'S VOICE
POWERFUL LESSONS IN PRAYER

HANNAH'S VOICE

POWERFUL LESSONS IN PRAYER

HANNAH'S VOICE

POWERFUL LESSONS IN PRAYER

BY

MINISTER ONEDIA N. GAGE

HANNAH'S VOICE

POWERFUL LESSONS IN PRAYER

SCRIPTURES

The Birth of Samuel

1 There was a certain man from Ramathaim, a Zuphite from the hill country of Ephraim, whose name was Elkanah son of Jeroham, the son of Elihu, the son of Tohu, the son of Zuph, an Ephraimite. ² He had two wives; one was called Hannah and the other Peninnah. Peninnah had children, but Hannah had none.

³ Year after year this man went up from his town to worship and sacrifice to the LORD Almighty at Shiloh, where Hophni and Phinehas, the two sons of Eli, were priests of the LORD. ⁴ Whenever the day came for Elkanah to sacrifice, he would give portions of the meat to his wife Peninnah and to all her sons and daughters. ⁵ But to Hannah he gave a double portion because he loved her, and the LORD had closed her womb. ⁶ Because the LORD had closed Hannah's womb, her rival kept provoking her in order to irritate her. ⁷ This went on year after year. Whenever Hannah went up to the house of the LORD, her rival provoked her till she wept and would not eat. ⁸ Her husband Elkanah would say to her, "Hannah, why are you weeping? Why don't you eat? Why are you downhearted? Don't I mean more to you than ten sons?"

⁹ Once when they had finished eating and drinking in Shiloh, Hannah stood up. Now Eli the priest was sitting on his chair by the doorpost of the LORD's house. ¹⁰ In her deep anguish Hannah prayed to the LORD, weeping bitterly. ¹¹ And she made a vow, saying, "LORD Almighty, if you will only look on your servant's misery and remember me, and not forget your servant but give her a son, then I will give him to the LORD for all the days of his life, and no razor will ever be used on his head."

HANNAH'S VOICE

[12] As she kept on praying to the LORD, Eli observed her mouth. [13] Hannah was praying in her heart, and her lips were moving but her voice was not heard. Eli thought she was drunk [14] and said to her, "How long are you going to stay drunk? Put away your wine."

[15] "Not so, my lord," Hannah replied, "I am a woman who is deeply troubled. I have not been drinking wine or beer; I was pouring out my soul to the LORD. [16] Do not take your servant for a wicked woman; I have been praying here out of my great anguish and grief."

[17] Eli answered, "Go in peace, and may the God of Israel grant you what you have asked of him."

[18] She said, "May your servant find favor in your eyes." Then she went her way and ate something, and her face was no longer downcast.

[19] Early the next morning they arose and worshiped before the LORD and then went back to their home at Ramah. Elkanah made love to his wife Hannah, and the LORD remembered her. [20] So in the course of time Hannah became pregnant and gave birth to a son. She named him Samuel, saying, "Because I asked the LORD for him."

Hannah Dedicates Samuel

[21] When her husband Elkanah went up with all his family to offer the annual sacrifice to the LORD and to fulfill his vow, [22] Hannah did not go. She said to her husband, "After the boy is weaned, I will take him and present him before the LORD, and he will live there always."

[23] "Do what seems best to you," her husband Elkanah told her. "Stay here until you have weaned him; only may the LORD make good his word." So the woman stayed at home and nursed her son until she had weaned him.

POWERFUL LESSONS IN PRAYER

^{24} After he was weaned, she took the boy with her, young as he was, along with a three-year-old bull, an ephah of flour and a skin of wine, and brought him to the house of the LORD at Shiloh. ^{25} When the bull had been sacrificed, they brought the boy to Eli, ^{26} and she said to him, "Pardon me, my lord. As surely as you live, I am the woman who stood here beside you praying to the LORD. ^{27} I prayed for this child, and the LORD has granted me what I asked of him. ^{28} So now I give him to the LORD. For his whole life he will be given over to the LORD." And he worshiped the LORD there.

Hannah's Prayer

2 Then Hannah prayed and said:

"My heart rejoices in the LORD;
   in the LORD my horn is lifted high.
My mouth boasts over my enemies,
   for I delight in your deliverance.
^{2} "There is no one holy like the LORD;
   there is no one besides you;
   there is no Rock like our God.
^{3} "Do not keep talking so proudly
   or let your mouth speak such arrogance,
for the LORD is a God who knows,
   and by him deeds are weighed.
^{4} "The bows of the warriors are broken,
   but those who stumbled are armed with strength.
^{5} Those who were full hire themselves out for food,
   but those who were hungry are hungry no more.

HANNAH'S VOICE

She who was barren has borne seven children,

    but she who has had many sons pines away.

[6] "The LORD brings death and makes alive;

    he brings down to the grave and raises up.

[7] The LORD sends poverty and wealth;

    he humbles and he exalts.

[8] He raises the poor from the dust

    and lifts the needy from the ash heap;

he seats them with princes

    and has them inherit a throne of honor.

"For the foundations of the earth are the LORD's;

    on them he has set the world.

[9] He will guard the feet of his faithful servants,

    but the wicked will be silenced in the place of darkness.

"It is not by strength that one prevails;

[10]   those who oppose the LORD will be broken.

The Most High will thunder from heaven;

    the LORD will judge the ends of the earth.

"He will give strength to his king

    and exalt the horn of his anointed."

[11] Then Elkanah went home to Ramah, but the boy ministered before the LORD under Eli the priest.

DEDICATION

Hillary

I pray for you.

You will need to pray.

Nehemiah

Because I prayed for you.

You will need to pray.

Prayer Warriors

We pray for others, then ourselves.

'Hannah'

Keep your focus on God.

Pray.

The Men who Hold the Hand of 'Hannah'

Pray.

Keep your focus on God.

Then her.

HANNAH'S VOICE

MORE BOOKS BY

MINISTER ONEDIA N. GAGE, PH. D.

Are You Ready for 9th Grade . . . Again? A Family's Guide to Success
As We Grow Together Daily Devotional for Expectant Couples
As We Grow Together Prayer Journal for Expectant Couples
As We Grow Together: Workbook for Expectant Couples Her Workbook
As We Grow Together: Workbook for Expectant Couples His Workbook
The Best 40 Days of Your Life: A Journey of Spiritual Renewal
The Blue Print: Poetry for the Soul
From Fat to Fit in 90 Days: A Fitness Journal
From Two to One: The Notebook for the Christian Couple
Her Story: The Legacy of Her Fight The Devotional
Her Story: The Legacy of Her Fight The Legacy Journal
Her Story: The Legacy of Her Fight Prayers and Journal
ILY! A Mother Daughter Relationship Workbook
In Her Own Words: Notebook for the Christian Woman
In Purple Ink: Poetry for the Spirit
The Intensive Retreat for Couples for Her
The Intensive Retreat for Couples for Him
Living a Whole Life: Sermons which Promote, Prompt and Provoke Life
Love Letters to God from a Teenage Girl
The Measure of a Woman: The Details of Her Soul
The Notebook: For Me, About Me, By Me
The Notebook for the Christian Teen
On This Journey Daily Devotional for Young People
On This Journey Prayer Journal for Young People
On This Journey Prayer Journal for Young People, Volume 2
One Day More Than We Deserve Prayer Journal for the Growing Christian
Promises, Promises: A Christian Novel
Queen in the Making: 30 Week Bible Study for Teen Girls
Tools for These Times: Timely Sermons for Uncertain Times
With An Anointed Voice: The Power of Prayer
Yielded and Submitted: A Woman's Journey for a Life Dedicated to God
Yielded and Submitted: A Woman's Journey for a Life Dedicated to God Intimate Study
Yielded and Submitted: A Woman's Journey for a Life Dedicated to God Prayers and Journal

HANNAH'S VOICE

LIBRARY OF CONGRESS

Hannah's Voice

Powerful Lessons in Prayer

All Rights Reserved © 2017

Rev. Onedia N. Gage

No part of this of book may be reproduced or transmitted in
Any form or by any means, graphic, electronic, or mechanical,
Including photocopying, recording, taping, or by any
Information storage or retrieval system, without the
Permission in writing from the publisher.

Purple Ink, Inc. Press

For Information address:
Purple Ink, Inc.
P O Box 300113
Houston, TX 77230

www.purpleink.net ♦ www.onediagage.com

onediagage@purpleink.net ♦ onediagage@onediagage.com

ISBN: 978-1-939119-57-5

Printed in the United States

DEAR GOD,

I thank You for Hannah and her prayer life! For every word she uttered and every word of it You shared with me, I thank You!

I pray that I can grow to have a prayer life that pleases You, My Rock and My Redeemer!

I ask You to bless the reader! I thank You for blessing the author.

Father God, thank You for the privilege of prayer. I thank You that I can come to You and leave with You ALL that ails me! Father God, thank You for a prayer warrior as an example in Jesus Christ. You sent Him and He taught us how to pray, when to pray, where to pray, and why we pray.

Lord God, finally thank You for Your Holy Spirit—the One You sent to intercede Your will on our behalf! Lord, I thank You and love You for all that You are and what You show me about myself.

Finally, God as I present my petitions to You with supplication and thanksgiving, I present them to You in the mighty name of Jesus Christ, with my whole heart!

Amen.

HANNAH'S VOICE

POWERFUL LESSONS IN PRAYER

DEAR SISTERS AND BROTHERS:

Prayer is our communication with God—Our God, Our Lord, Our Rock, Our Redeemer, Our Forgiver, and Our Definition of Love.

The power of prayer is what God offers us to seek Him with all that we are—feeble and unable. However, He is able and diligent and willing and loving and forgiving and AWESOME!

The problem with prayer is that we do not pray. We do not pray regularly. We do not pray with faith and expectation. We do not pray unless something is wrong and we are at rock bottom.

We often pray with the wrong motives. We are certainly beggars and benefit driven. We are considerably out of the will of God regarding prayer.

Hannah shows us how to invite the Lord into our situation and give Him the control that already belonged to Him. Ultimately, she teaches surrender to Him all that we are and all that we have.

Let Hannah be a reminder that we are God's workmanship and He can do whatever He likes. We need to be submissive and surrendered so that we can do His will.

He loves us and has demonstrated it a hundred times over . . . today!

Pray? Pray. Pray!

In God's Service,

Onedia N. Gage

Rev. Onedia N. Gage

HANNAH'S VOICE

TABLE OF CONTENTS

Scripture

Dedication

Prayer

Letter

SERMONS

A Calling Like Hannah's	23
Hannah Teaches the Rejection of Revenge	33
Hannah Teaches Focus on God	39
Hannah Teaches Surrender to God	49
Hannah Teaches Service to God	59
Hannah Teaches Obedience to God	67
Hannah Teaches How to Seek God with Zeal	75
Hannah Prays Fervently	85
Hannah Gives Sound Advice	95
Hannah Shares Valuable Insight	105
Acknowledgements	117
About the Prayer Warrior	119

HANNAH'S VOICE

HANNAH'S VOICE: POWERFUL LESSONS IN PRAYER

HANNAH'S VOICE

POWERFUL LESSONS IN PRAYER

A Calling Like Hannah's

1 Samuel 1:1-5

[1] There was a certain man from Ramathaim, a Zuphite from the hill country of Ephraim, whose name was Elkanah son of Jeroham, the son of Elihu, the son of Tohu, the son of Zuph, an Ephraimite. [2] He had two wives; one was called Hannah and the other Peninnah. Peninnah had children, but Hannah had none. [3] Year after year this man went up from his town to worship and sacrifice to the LORD Almighty at Shiloh, where Hophni and Phinehas, the two sons of Eli, were priests of the LORD. [4] Whenever the day came for Elkanah to sacrifice, he would give portions of the meat to his wife Peninnah and to all her sons and daughters. [5] But to Hannah he gave a double portion because he loved her, and the LORD had closed her womb.

Lord God, afresh I thank You for this day for what You have in store for us for our ten-part study of Hannah. We thank You right now Lord, that You give us exactly what it is we need this day to go forward, and come into the complete and total understanding of what it is You want for us to learn, take from this day and be rejuvenated, revived and be taken unto Yourself. Lord God, we thank You afresh today for what we'll learn, and what we'll embrace, and what we'll understand, and what we'll take away immediately from You, Lord God. Lord, we'll discover a calling like Hannah's. Lord, we thank You for what You do in this conversation through us. Lord, forgive me of all my sins and unworthiness. And we also want to pray for any women who this is their story – women with a closed womb; that they feel the way that they do because they haven't borne children. So Lord, we thank You right now and in Your Son Jesus' name, we pray. Amen.

Sermon

Hannah is very special for many reasons, so we're going to explore Hannah through 1 Samuel chapter 1 through chapter 2. In the study of Hannah, we will

HANNAH'S VOICE

discover a few things. We will start with "A Calling Like Hannah's." I'm very excited that there's a special calling like Hannah's, because God doesn't call just anybody to do anything. He calls each of us to do special things.

Inside of those special things, He gives us an opportunity to do greatness for Him if only we will be obedient and reject revenge, understand how to pull together our complete and total surrender to Him. For Hannah, He gives her special lessons, and we will uncover those special lessons through her. Hannah is a very special woman that is designed to give us a lot of information, in a very short period of time.

By all societal measures, a woman with a closed womb, unable to have children, has a not so noble role in society. With this position being the situation, we want to make sure we give due consideration of the feelings and values and self-worth that comes from these types of conversations. That's the first thing – we want to hear from their heart the measure that they feel they're worth based on how they feel about themselves, because of their inability to have children.

So assuming that Hannah – and we're not far enough along in the scripture to know, did not feel good about herself, because she was not able to bear Elkanah [her husband] children. There is a special calling on Hannah's life. Hannah is going to walk through some steps, and we're going to walk through those steps for the next nine sermons, as to what she did in regards to her challenge, her calling.

Her calling has several implications. The first being that there are things that God gives us that are considered stumbling blocks or obstacles, in order to get our attention. It gives us the opportunity to focus on Him. This is a simple test as a bystander. It is simple test of how authentic is your worship, and how committed to God is your praise and prayer life. This is a simple thing. One of the things that we have to look at from Hannah's calling is that Hannah had to endure a few things in the next few verses. Her behavior let us know that she had a praise and worship for God.

God cannot call everyone to do the things He called Hannah to do. God has a knack for picking certain women to birth certain children. He has a knack for that. You must understand that, without much ado – Hannah is the mother of Samuel. Mary is the mother of Jesus; Elizabeth is the mother of John the Baptist. It's understood that God picks some very special women, and He gives boys to them, under some very unique circumstances, and once He gives boys to them under these very unique circumstances – these become great men.

So, in order to know if we will do the things that God has called upon us to do, and enable us to be the women He needs us to be, to be the parent to that particular young man that He has birthed within us, He gives us some special circumstances to overcome. Now in this situation, Hannah has a closed womb, and in order for Hannah to get from A to B, she has a lot of midpoints…a lot of little points to overcome. First of all, she has to overcome her husband's other wife, Peninnah, and her ability to have children.

The next thing that she has to overcome is being perceived as drunk by the priest, Eli, as she's trying to pray. The third thing is that she makes a very obtuse promise to God, if you will. In spite of this prayer, most of us would have forgotten what we said. However, not only did Hannah not forget what she said, she also kept her word, and God honored her by leaving her womb open and she bore many children after this point.

Not just be anybody can be the mother of Samuel. Just like how you can't be any regular woman to be the mother of our Savior Jesus Christ. Nor could you be any regular woman to be the mother of John the Baptist who led the way for Jesus, and baptized Jesus.

HANNAH'S VOICE

You have to engage in some self-reflection and say, "Who does it have to be that woman He chooses for these types of assignments? Am I going to be able to do this magnitude of work? How can I communicate the following: I am going to be this person. I'm going to be worthy. Jesus can trust me. Jesus can trust me with this assignment." Now, we don't necessarily know that we have set out on this type of assignment or that we have embarked on this type of journey or that we've been called into this level of assignment, until most of us are already in it.

Hannah had no idea what she was about to embark upon. Because God knows everything, is everywhere, and has plans for our lives – and nothing that He does is without a purpose or point or a plan, we already know that when He closed her womb it was an exercise on what can He do? And what will He do? And in which fashion will He get it done? You see, we don't necessarily need a hint or a shove to remind us what kind of God He is; what kind of God we serve. We don't necessarily need that. We don't need that to happen. What we do need to understand is that when He gives us an assignment, we need to be anticipating the assignment; such a hearty assignment. We need to be anticipating it at any time, and we need to be ready for it at all times. Any step is toward an assignment at any given moment.

We want to mention at this moment that Elkanah loved his wife, and he never intended for it to go this way. For all his sacrifices, he gave her a double portion. Because he loved her, he's compassionate to her situation. He showed her that he's not going to ignore her situation, her scenario. He wants her to understand that he's going to give her of himself in such a manner that when he gives of himself to her, she's aware that he's compassionate to her. So understand that she's got a calling on her life. She's going to have a special assignment, straight from God, to do a very special thing: give birth to Samuel. Later, we will discuss that she made some very heavy promises to God, promises that the Word said that she fully keeps.

POWERFUL LESSONS IN PRAYER

What we want to be sure of though is that when she keeps her word, she gives an ultimate sacrifice back to God. That's what He wants to know: if He gives you something you've asked for, will you give it back to Him? Will you share it with Him the way that you said that you would? Is there any way that you can give to God what He's already given to you: can you give it back? He may not want it; He just wants to know if you'll give it to him... will you give it up? All that you ever ask for will you give it back to Him? Because He asked for it back.

Abraham had that opportunity with Isaac. Because God said, "I want you to go and sacrifice Isaac." And just as Abraham had pulled back the axe and was just about to lay it down to sacrifice his son Isaac, the Lord said, "Don't put a hand on him. There's a ram in the bush."

So understand that the Lord wants to know what we'll do with what He has given us. Will we use our talents properly? Will we do what it is that He says for us to do? A calling like Hannah's is hard. There are women around the world who cannot have children, and they feel like it as a personal affront to their femininity; their self-esteem is very low. In order to have compassion for that woman, you've got to be very close to her or you also have to have a likeness of situation.

No one wants to talk about it: it's a social stigma. Every woman should have been born able to have children. Yet, that is not so. There are women who struggle tremendously through the process of bearing children. The process of conceiving a child, and the process of carrying the child once that child is planted inside of her womb. Give yourself an opportunity to understand that woman, from her vantage point. Some women think that the only purpose of being a woman is to have a baby. They think that's the only difference between us and men. Now, while I wholeheartedly disagree with that statement, I will stand with another woman in order to be compassionate to her, for her plight in this life. I will stand with her because we don't know what her calling is in this situation.

I have a friend, who doesn't have her own children, and her sister passed away, so she became their mother. Her nephews became her children. What if she had had children? Would she have room in her home and her heart, her attitude and disposition to take in additional children? That begs the question: Is that why she didn't have her own children? Is it because she was held available with a closed womb to take care of her sister's children? And then to take it a bit further, will He then use this child whose mother has nurtured her children and then passed away, then how will He bless her sister?

You've got to give that some credence and consideration, because God can do it. He did it with Elizabeth. She was barren and she was up in age, the Word said. However, she gave birth to a healthy boy, leaping within her womb – John the Baptist. She has a very finite time that she spends on Earth with him. Yet, he had a very profound ministry, very profound ministry. So when we consider what our role in life is, what the calling is of our lives, we have to understand that God makes provisions for that calling.

God takes that calling to a level where we have to be responsible for what He's calling us to do. The Lord is calling us to do some things for some people in some timeframes that may not suit our desires. Don't you think she was questioning God? Yes, she goes on to do that, and we'll unpack that at a later time, but she goes on to say some things and asks some questions, but prays mightily. She actually employs an intercessor, and asks that intercessor to plead to God for her situation, to plead her case to the Lord. At that point in time, she has to convince someone else; she has to sell her story to another human being, who has no idea of which she speaks.

Ask yourself, "Are you certain? Have you considered a calling as a challenge?"

1. Are you certain that you'll recognize your challenge as a calling?

2. Have you addressed your challenge and your calling with the type of attention that only God deserves?

3. Are there those around you who recognize that you're in this challenge, perhaps this calling, and they have compassion on your situation?

You see oftentimes, we get embarrassed so we don't want to tell anyone that we stand in need of something. We don't tell them when we stand in need of something, and because we don't tell them that we stand in need of something, or a problem that we have, no one can help us because they don't know that we are in pain. Pride will do that to us. The asking may not just be for you, but the person you're asking it of, so they can grow and they can do some things as well. Ask yourself, "When I am put in a position where I meet other people, how many people are learning from that situation?" It may be more than you realize.

So we understand that there's a calling now, there's a challenge as given by God to move us.

Now, when we consider the calling on Hannah's life and we consider those things that God has done that may be a little off, or a little weird, or a whole lot of uncomfortable in our lives – what are we supposed to do with that? We answer Him with our actions and a great attitude.

So in 1998, God called me to preach, and I was highly uncomfortable with that role. Not something I've ever been accustomed to: being uncomfortable. I've never been particularly uncomfortable with anything, but God challenged me – He called me in order to have me preach. I made a phone call to my pastor immediately and told him what was going on. He said, "Well, that sounds like a calling to preach to me."

Oh I didn't like that. I didn't want that to be the case. I wanted him to say something else. I wanted him to have doubt, or discouragement to keep from pursuing it as I heard it but he did not. I reconciled with myself thinking, 'God really was not calling me to preach; He was calling me to continue to teach and prepare better. Amen. That's great.' He was calling me to my writing – that all my writing be Christian writing. 'Don't delve into the secular world at that level.' 'Yes, I can do that. As a matter of fact, I can edit this book at this moment.'

Five years later in 2003, the Lord got my attention again, and He said, "Lady, I made you to preach, and I'm not asking you. This is not a conversation; this is a command." And I said, "Yes sir." From that day in 2003 and from the 1998 conversation, I've resolved in my mind that while my calling has been a challenge, I will follow and preach. My family has rejected my calling. My peers have rejected my calling. Other people misunderstand the whole point of God calling women into a preaching ministry. Remember that God can use whomever He wants to do whatever He wants that pleases Him. God picks those of us who are going to follow the will that He has set forth.

That's what He's going to do. He didn't pick people who are not going to get themselves together. He did not pick people who are not going to get their act in line. when He gets your attention of a calling that you have, it could be something as simple as closing a womb, and something as devastating as blinding you for three days. Your job is to put yourself in a position so that when He calls you, and He challenges you, you can answer His call immediately. We want to give God time that is of quality.

That is His expectation. We want to take those challenges and callings to be one of those things where we say, "God has called and challenged me." That translates into He trusts me, or He wants to trust me. That He's in pursuit of me and all that He has created me to be. So with this calling and this challenge we are commissioned to come forward, and to stand in sight of the will of God — do the very things that God has called us to do. There is no way around what we are called to do. There is no getting out of it. God is going to get the glory regardless. What you don't want to do is miss an opportunity for God to use you.

Remember that Hannah could have reacted differently, so we'll talk about the things that she did. Her disposition could have been one of hatred and strife and disdain. Those characteristics are not the characteristics of the mother of the kind of person Samuel is. So we have to ask ourselves, "If Hannah had acted in that manner, would God have used someone else or would Hannah's behavior cause the Lord to change the timeframe in order to get Hannah onboard?"

How would God have solved that problem? Understand that God can get your attention. God is very good at getting our attention. He gets our attention in such a way that it strikes at the very heart of the matter. He's going to give us a very positively signature move. It takes God to get your attention. It takes Him to get our attention. God can do it in ways no one else can. Nor will they ever do.

We have to recognize our calling. We have to recognize that our calling is going to be considered a challenge. We have to remember that we're commissioned with that type of trust because it is what He has for us. So consider your life and ask yourself, "What is He calling me to do? What is He calling on me for? What is it that He's expecting of me?" And with that being said, start paying attention to all the things that He shares with you, and shows you.

HANNAH'S VOICE

Start looking around for the things that He has for you. You want to be sure that you understand that. You want to be clear that you understand His mechanism, and His methods. And while you won't completely comprehend them, know that they apply to your behavior.

Lord God, we thank You afresh for this word, His might and its power to infuse joy within for the things that You're doing in each of our lives. Our calling, our challenges, and our commissions. We thank You for a life like Hannah's. We thank You for Hannah and her obedience. We thank You for her son Samuel, and we give You all the honor, glory and praise. It is in Your exalted name that we ask it all. Amen.

POWERFUL LESSONS IN PRAYER

HANNAH TEACHES THE REJECTION OF REVENGE

1 Samuel 1:6-7

[6] Because the LORD had closed Hannah's womb, her rival kept provoking her in order to irritate her. [7] This went on year after year. Whenever Hannah went up to the house of the LORD, her rival provoked her till she wept and would not eat.

SERMON

There is show on ABC called Revenge. As a secular society, we have become accustomed to the nature of revenge. We are accustomed to revenge. We take revenge so seriously and we make things happens which is not okay. It happened in the Bible and it happens daily. The Bible also speaks to the point of not taking revenge on others. Revenge belongs to the Lord. Leviticus 19:18 (NIV) reads: "[18]Do not seek revenge or bear a grudge against anyone among your people, but love your neighbor as yourself. I am the LORD."

We are going to look at Hannah's story with the attitude that we are to reject revenge. We want to consider the option of ignoring the events and people which would cause us to be revengeful.

Hannah had every right to retaliate against Peninah, the other wife, because Peninah tried to provoke Hannah. Just picking on her. Rubbing her lack of motherhood in her face. You know how that is for someone to just constantly remind you of what you are not, in spite of who you want to be. Peninah had children, but Hannah did not. She wanted children because of the culture's validation of woman is through childbirth. She thinks that she cannot be the woman she is supposed to be without children. In the first five verses, her husband gives her a double portion when they go to worship and sacrifice because of his compassion for her and her barrenness.

HANNAH'S VOICE

Her rival keeps provoking her. When someone is consistently prodding you, against you, and instigating you; someone you are in competition with, someone you are being compared to, someone you are not aligned with because you should be rivaled and enemies.

How do you have time to provoke another woman? You have much work to do. You really do not have time for that. Don't you have children and a husband to care for? Now that you have found time to provoke her, what is your motivation to do so? Why are you so inclined to provoke her? What keeps you provoking her? Why can't you be compassionate? In my mind's eye, in order for you to provoke me, and cause me to respond, I have to discontent about something. There is something that motivates that. I have to be jealous enough of you or find something valuable enough about you to provoke you, not because of something that I have that you do not. So I am baffled about why you would provoke someone based on what you have, rather than what they have?

So it begs the question what does Peninah find so valuable about Hannah that she keeps this going and gives her this type of time and attention? If I find you to provoke you, then I need a reason to provoke you. It requires a lot of energy; energy I can use for something really productive. So what were the motivating factors: was Hannah smart, respected, well-liked? Was she the first wife? Did Elkanah give her more attention? Talked very highly of her? Did he value her more? Was it that Hannah got the double portion? And Peninah was not? What exactly got Peninah's attention? What caused this activity to start and to continue? What was in Peninah's heart?

If I wanted children, then it seems like I would be the provoker of Peninah. But that is not the road that Hannah took. Hannah takes what is referred to as the high road. On that high road, Hannah does not respond. Not to her, and not the way the average person would respond. Hannah is not drawn into the situation as is.

When you take the role of a provoker, you then position yourself as the enemy, the adversary, then you use all of that motivation to irritate her. What does it take to do all of that? I am concerned that you would spend time irritating someone. So much irritation that it is mentioned in the Bible. We know that she is irritated but what is the rest of the story. She decides what she will do next. Because she has to decide what to do and inside of this choice is the ability to ignore.

Hannah exercises her ability to ignore. She does this through prayer. When she decides to do this through prayer, she takes an elevated understanding. In this culture and time, more than one wife is allowed. In our current culture, this is unacceptable. Our current situation is subject to what we have going on at the time. What would we do if we were in Hannah's situation? This scenario exists and maybe even in a worst situation. Imagine the wife who cannot get pregnant and he has a child from a previous or a new outside relationship. There could be some provocation there.

What would you do? Jesus said that if your enemy slaps your cheek, give him the other one as well. Hannah is in a different mindset. Her scripture is 'vengeance is mine said the Lord.' We would handle that much differently. We would have responded with ugly words and threatened to cause bodily harm, possibly filed legal documents. She would have been confronted. She would been addressed. The husband would have been confronted also.

Hannah does not do any of those things. Hannah recognizes that God closed her womb which means that this was not about her. Secondly, Hannah has a special favor with her husband that Peninah seemingly does not have. Peninah may recognize that favor and is jealous of that. Although she has been classified as a

HANNAH'S VOICE

woman by child birth, does her husband validate and esteem her as a woman? I believe he does.

What is God doing in this scenario? God is demonstrating His trust in Hannah. He knows how Peninah, Elkanah, and even Hannah will behave. He is now showing her how much He does trust her. Eventually, He will share with the rest of us. It takes a lot for a woman with a closed womb to look up rather than down or around. It takes a special woman to have a closed womb. The self-esteem of most women is wrapped around their children's lives, clothes, and activities. They live through their lives and exist to talk about their kids and their activities. They do everything for them. When the child goes to college, the mom does not have a life. She gave it away when she had the child. She gave up the definition of herself for the child.

God wants to know will she give Me up for the child or will she love Me fervently like she always has. We can tell that being provoked hurt her. She wept, she would not eat, she probably could not sleep and she was probably not very social. She was not angry; she was hurt. She was deeply wounded. She was very embittered in this season.

Several questions might come up such as 'Why me, Lord?' His answer is usually, 'Why not you?' 'Will this ever change?' is the second of such questions. 'What would You have me to do in the meantime while I wait on You to open up my womb? While I wait on You to answer me?' is the third question. 'Why are you letting her provoke me during my misfortune? You gave me this misfortune, and that is fine, but why would You let someone provoke me in the meantime?' is the next conversation. 'Why would You let that happen? Why would You allow that to take place? Why would You let be the case?' follows.

The lesson that Hannah teaches is to ignore the rival, prepare for the calling and what God has for us to do, and anticipate some outstanding results. It is super hard to ignore, especially when you want to respond. We must ignore such rivals, we must ignore that desire. We must ignore the haters and all those who mean you complete and utter harm. If we do not ignore them, then what will God say to us? What will God have to do to clean up our mess when we respond inappropriately? We have to give some real consideration toward how we will control ourselves during this adversity. Joseph dealt with this as well. His response to his brothers was Genesis 50:20, "[20] You intended to harm me, but God intended it for good to accomplish what is now being done, the saving of many lives."

When Hannah teaches the rejection of revenge, we need to view ourselves as being focused on the plan. We need to focus so that we please God. So that means we are going to ask God for help, ask Him to cover us, seek our needs through Him, we are going to check in with Him via prayer, and we are going to share with Him how we feel. We will ignore them and since this is part of God's plan and is not personal to us, we are going to let Him handle it. Exodus 14:14 reads: "He will fight my battles if I just be still."

We need to address Hannah's weeping moment. It would be presumed that she felt sorry for herself because she would not eat. If she is anything like us, she wept because she was not in control and she realized that. She is like many of us who are upset when we do not have the solution and the only solution is God. She wept out of desire to accomplish what she had set her mind to. God put all of that on pause. He wants her to participate by His rules and on His timing.

Lastly, Hannah teaches us to develop the understanding that we have the opportunity to seek God. We have the opportunity to move away from the issue and current environment. Do we make that choice? Not always. Do we make that happen? Not always.

HANNAH'S VOICE

The rejection of revenge is real. We have to ignore our rival and those things that irritate us. We have to keep our eye on God: we have to seek Him. We have to get into a place where we can hear from God.

Amen.

POWERFUL LESSONS IN PRAYER

HANNAH TEACHES FOCUS ON GOD

1 Samuel 1:8-11

⁸ Her husband Elkanah would say to her, "Hannah, why are you weeping? Why don't you eat? Why are you downhearted? Don't I mean more to you than ten sons?"

⁹ Once when they had finished eating and drinking in Shiloh, Hannah stood up. Now Eli the priest was sitting on his chair by the doorpost of the LORD's house. ¹⁰ In her deep anguish Hannah prayed to the LORD, weeping bitterly. ¹¹ And she made a vow, saying, "LORD Almighty, if you will only look on your servant's misery and remember me, and not forget your servant but give her a son, then I will give him to the LORD for all the days of his life, and no razor will ever be used on his head."

SERMON

A little background about this scene, Hannah wants to have a son. In this time period, a woman's validation as a woman is based on having a baby, specifically a son. She has been barren. She goes before the Lord to petition for that son. She promises a profound promise. She sets the stage for how promises are made to God with the accountability to keep that promise.

Hannah was near the place of worship. She was visible to Eli. He witnessed her outcry to God. At this point, she has totally surrendered. She encounters Eli. Hannah is weeping so her husband seeks to comfort her and seeks his own validation with a question of 'am I not enough.' She never answers him, according to the text, however, the answer is obviously no because she continues to pursue God for this son. The additional issue is that she does feel complete as

HANNAH'S VOICE

the wife she wants to be for Elkanah because she does not feel whole. That is a different lesson for a different message.

Hannah's focus is on God. In her whole being, her whole person, she is weeping bitterly. Our first response to bitterness is to pray. In her darkest hour, by her own definition, and at her lowest point, her response is to pray and is designed to show the Lord what she needs and what she wants. The text states that she was weeping bitterly which translates into serious and important. It means she has been hurting for a long time. We do not weep bitterly over minor things. We do not weep bitterly about something which can be solved in an afternoon. We weep bitterly when there is not a complete amount of hope, while we still have faith in God. We weep bitterly because God could say no and if He does, we understand that we have done our part. We have submitted our concerns to God. We are supposed to leave our burdens with God.

In our deepest anguish and in our darkest hour and in our worst of times, we are still supposed to pray. God still expects to hear from us in our prayer time with Him. He is listening to us at all times. He knows exactly where we are. He knows exactly what we are underneath. He knows exactly what we are going through. None of this will be new to God. Most importantly is how we handle our challenges. At some point, we all have had something to say to God. We all have voiced our opinions to God about our challenges. We have asked to be excused from the lesson and the experience just for the purpose of being excused. We have asked to miss this lesson because we do not want to be inconvenienced by this lesson.

However, Hannah teaches us that she knows that she is still a servant of God. She demonstrates that God is in control and is still in charge of her: 'I am still under Your hand. You are still in charge of me.' This is focus on God. This is a not being distracted by her husband because of his questions. How does Elkanah feel when Hannah does not answer him? Did he feel disrespected? She does not stop her pursuit of God. She has God's attention.

What takes my focus off of God? This is the question. Similar situations take our focus off of God. The mate does not mean any harm but we need to consider what they are saying when they seek to provide comfort through phrases such as 'you do not need all of that,' 'it does not take all of that,' and tries to provide a solution which does not investigate the real lesson and does not drive you directly to God. If the solution does not include God or does not involve seeking God or referring to what God has already said, then we are not focused on God. We are supposed to be focused on God. More importantly, we are supposed to want to be focused on God. God asks for a certain amount of attention from each of us. God has already told us that He is a jealous God. We cannot afford not to give our best at all times. That is a dangerous situation to be in.

At all times, we need to be in a place where God knows that we are focused on Him, where we know that we are focused on Him, and where all people around us and even those at a distance, know that we are focused on Him. That focus should be recognized by others as well. Hannah does just that.

The way the scripture text is written, we know that Hannah is not alone. Hannah is in public place. Her prayer is not a secret. Jesus teaches us in Matthew 6 that we are not to pray in public to get the attention of others. We will revisit this later to discuss how Hannah uses this to serve the Lord. Hannah is showing us how to focus on God. As Hannah shows us how to focus on God, Hannah does not leave anything undone. She does it with excellence.

The second aspect that Hannah teaches is that her disposition and attitude does not stop her from approaching God. First, she knew it was what she was supposed to do. Secondly, she did what she was supposed to do. It is one thing to know what to do. It is another level of obedience, reverence and respect to do

HANNAH'S VOICE

exactly what you were supposed to do. She goes into prayer, and while praying she makes a vow to God, a promise. Verse 11 reads, "And she made a vow, saying, "LORD Almighty, if You will only look on Your servant's misery and remember me, and not forget Your servant but give her a son, then I will give him to the LORD for all the days of his life, and no razor will ever be used on his head."

She makes a big promise in her prayer. This is serious. This is bold. She is committed to her need. She is determined for her petition to be heard. Inside of that request she does something profound. When we make promises to God, we are accountable for those promises. We are accountable for all of that we said we would do. Just like we want God to keep His promises, we have to keep ours. There was a contingency given, 'if You do this for me, God, I will do ____ _____ for You.' We were supposed to do something to bring God glory, however we normally forget that which we promised. We forget conveniently to complete the deal.

It is very inappropriate to make that promise when you do not know if you have the sustainability to keep that promise. These promises are made out of desperation and with good intentions, however, we often do not have the ability to maintain that promise. 'I vow.' That is a conditional statement. 'If You will only…' That has conditions. What happens if we do not hold up our end of the bargain? When we talk about Hannah's focus on God, we need to consider Hannah's history with God. What is Hannah's track record with promises? Should she be allowed this request based on her previous behavior?

That is what we need to investigate for ourselves about our requests. Do we represent ourselves well enough for God to feel comfortable enough to give us what we are asking God for? What is our track record for these promises? Clearly, some of the things we are asking God for will take our focus off of God.

POWERFUL LESSONS IN PRAYER

Is that the best idea for God? Will we keep our focus on Him after He gives us our requests? Sometimes the answer is no. Most of all when we are praying to God, when we are giving Him all that we are, when we are focused on God, when we are giving all that we know that we have to offer, are we doing it for the right reasons and with the correct motives?

When we consider Hannah's request: I will give him over to You, does she know about the calling on Samuel's life? Does she know anything about the man that Samuel will become? Does she know what God has in store for him? We cannot answer that question. We should raise an eyebrow though. When we are negotiating deals with God, do we know what God has planned? The answer is no. We do not have the foggiest notion or idea about what God will do next or why this would be beneficial to His plan or if it falls within His will. We do not know how we fit into His plans. We do not know how our plans would contradict or sabotage or derail His plans if He granted some of these requests we hand to Him. We have no idea. That is why He says no. That is why our negotiations do not work.

When we consider Hannah's focus, she pleads for relief from her misery. God did not co-sign on this misery. God does not agree that she exists in misery. When Elkanah went to her, he presented himself as important to her, more important than what she has labeled as important. She rejected that comfort. She was challenged about what was important.

Doesn't God show us that from time to time? Won't He remove things and people from us to remind us that what we have labeled as important is not what He defined as important? God will take things from us which has removed our focus away from Him. When we are away from Him and out of focus, He does some of those things to get our attention. When He regains our attention, He can then let us know what He wants from us. When we say that we need to be closer to God, there are people, places and things we will need to let go. There are events which are going to happen so that He can show us what it really means to be closer to Him; what it looks like, how it feels, and what it consists of.

When we are focused on God, how bold do we need to be? Well, let us look at Hannah once again. Hannah is really bold. Hannah says, 'if You will remember me.' She had waited to have a baby. She kept watching others have babies. She did not get as anxious as Sarah had but she had been taunted so she was getting impatient. Yet, she kept praying. She had been praying for a very long time. Her prayers have not been answered. She was almost desperate.

I believe that she knew that God would not give her that baby if He thought or knew that she would lose focus on God. Why would He do that? He would not. There is no way that God would give you something that would keep your focus off of Him and you get to keep it. I cannot fathom that it would happen. God is selfish. He makes that extremely clear. He is not jealous on occasion and under certain circumstances—He is jealous all of the time. I believe that she knew that.

Where in your life do you need to focus on Him? What part of your life is out of sync regarding Him? What are you asking for? Is that request going to take your focus off of God? We need to ask ourselves those questions on a daily basis.

How do we lose our focus on God? Let us examine the before and after request behavior. If before you were employed at that job, were you attending church more or less than you do now? Is the job affecting your church attendance? Are you serving at church with the same or better than you did before the new house or car? Did the way you served God change based on what you were blessed with? Are you doing the things you would have been doing except that you have these extra hours that you have to work? Is this job preventing you from being in church on a regular basis or making it difficult to do so?

POWERFUL LESSONS IN PRAYER

Can you figure what your focus measurement is? Can you figure out that 'this' takes me and my focus away from God so I should not do that? Can you discern that 'this' draws me closer to God, so I definitely want to do that? Can you independently determine that or do you need God to bring it to your attention? Can you make it happen?

I am concerned about what we are trying to get accomplished in this world. What we cannot seem to get done is to take the charge to focus on God. Being focused on God means that you do what God desires regardless of the situation. Focus on God means that you still complete the task regardless of the situation and the conditions.

Hannah didn't get discouraged and Hannah did not get anxious. Hannah did not get disturbed or distraught and forgot that she was on assignment for God; that she belongs to Him. Hannah was bold and took action. She went before the Lord and pleaded her case. She did not stop worshiping, praising or working. She was honest with God. She made a deal with God that said if you would allow me to have a baby boy, then You can have this baby boy back. Notice she was very specific: she asked for a boy, not just a baby.

What is crazy about this whole deal is whether or not you can be trusted. What is your track record? Can you be trusted with the promises you make? Can God believe you for your promises? So when He does not give us some of the things we ask for, is it because He doesn't believe you will keep your word? Is your word worth anything? Are you really going to keep your word? Focus on God requires being trusted by God. We keep our word. We keep our promises. We can be held accountable for exactly what He says and wants us to do. He needs to be able to trust us.

We need to ask ourselves is she capable of keeping her word. She extended that promise to something that was not in her control. Verse 11 says, 'then I will give

HANNAH'S VOICE

him to the LORD for all the days of his life.' She made a committed for an unconceived child. She promised that the unconceived baby would belong to God all the days of his life. This child has not been conceived, is not born, and is not here. We cannot control those who are here much less those who are not. We cannot determine what most of our children are going to do from one minute to the next but Hannah promised for the rest of his life; something she has no control over, but she promises him with zest and zeal and conviction of heart. She is committed and she has committed him as well. She does not even know that the character of the child will help her to uphold the promise she has made. She does not waiver. She does not stammer. She charges ahead. The promise she makes is permanent and without hesitation. She will give God what belongs to Him. She did not promise that she would take him to church, rather that he would already be there. She did not promise to baptize him, instead the church would have control over that. She did not give God 10% or some other portion, but she gave God all that belonged to him: the whole baby. 'If you validate me in the fashion by allowing me to have the child, you can have him back. I don't need him; I just want to know that I can have a child,' Hannah's thoughts.

Don't we do that? For all of us this would not have been the case, we want our cake and we want to eat it too. We would not have been able to give it up. Imagine that you have waited for this baby but you promised him to the Lord. You would be trying to justify your desire to renege on the promise.

Hannah made a second commitment: No razor would ever be used on his head. Wow! What a commitment for an unconceived, unborn child. Her vow has to be kept even though he will grow up and be his own man. That is a risk. That is a bold proposition. But her focus to God was so serious, so stern, and so committed that she was all in. She never planned to excuse herself from her commitment, even after he was grown and fully capable of making his own decisions. She was all in and committed to him being in God's hands for his

POWERFUL LESSONS IN PRAYER

lifetime. Her actions say out loud that 'I will not let him cut his hair and he will serve You all the days of his life.' She committed something to God that she does not control. That is trust. You can read ahead to understand how the rest of the story ends. How and when will she tell this son that he cannot put a razor to his head?

I believe because of her commitment, her boldness, seeking God in her time of anguish and deep depression, being able to be focused on God through her storm, offering her praise to God, being authentic in that prayer, and being able to deliver on her promise is how she was blessed. Her blessings came from that. She was blessed with a whole group of kids. But she gave Samuel to God just as she said that she would.

I believe that our focus on God is what causes us to be a mighty blessing. Hannah had to give of herself. Hannah gave up her first born without any regrets or abandonment issues or misgivings or hesitation or questions. She kept her word: a Woman of Integrity. She said, 'I will give you the baby that You gave me.' As soon as she was able to take that baby, she took that baby to the temple and left him with Eli, the priest. How did her marriage improve?

As you read on, you can find out fantastic, wonderful and profound a man of God that Samuel became. But he was the man who was all started with a vow made by a little lady who just wanted to be a mom.

My question for you today as we consider our focus on God is your conviction for God that strong? Is your faith that strong and sturdy so that you can go before the Lord with that level of boldness and say that I will still acknowledge the Lord, that I will handle Your business, that I will still be zealous for You, even if I do not receive what it is that I have requested? Because the Lord, our God, is a loving God and He is righteous. He has not forgotten about us. Our concerns are important to Him.

HANNAH'S VOICE

Hannah's story inspires me, it convicts me, it convinces me, it coerces me into a better behavior. Hannah teaches me to focus on God.

In golf, you keep your head down and keep your eye on the ball. You never look away from the ball until you actually hit the ball. Don't look away from the ball for any reason. If you look away, you may miss the ball, and more importantly, you will miss your intended target. And therein lies a lesson for each of us, as long as I keep my focus on God, everything else is added unto me. As soon as I take my eyes off of God, things start to unravel, mistakes are made, issues arise unexpectedly and because I have my eyes and heart diverted from God, I am underprepared and ill-equipped.

What is it that I am doing that needs His attention and His focus? What does God want me to focus on? If we are not asking those questions authentically, then we need to ask ourselves why that is. God is not our cosmic bellhop. God is our Creator, who deserves our reverence and respect, regardless of our storm or situation or circumstance or dilemma; or moodiness. It does not matter your storm, it is what you owe God. It does not matter that He did not honor your request and give you what you wanted. You don't know what He protected you from when He said no.

Hannah teaches us that focus, and that transparency with God. I pray that you consider that God looked at her heart and its intentions. He certainly searches our hearts with every request.

POWERFUL LESSONS IN PRAYER

HANNAH TEACHES SURRENDER TO GOD

1 Samuel 1:12-17

[12] As she kept on praying to the LORD, Eli observed her mouth. [13] Hannah was praying in her heart, and her lips were moving but her voice was not heard. Eli thought she was drunk [14] and said to her, "How long are you going to stay drunk? Put away your wine."

[15] "Not so, my lord," Hannah replied, "I am a woman who is deeply troubled. I have not been drinking wine or beer; I was pouring out my soul to the LORD. [16] Do not take your servant for a wicked woman; I have been praying here out of my great anguish and grief."

[17] Eli answered, "Go in peace, and may the God of Israel grant you what you have asked of him."

SERMON

Surrender is defined by dictionary.com as "to yield (something, such as yourself) to the possession or power of another; to yield or resign in favor of another."

Hannah's story is one that most would view as sad. Hannah is married but does not have any children. She so desperately wants a child. She begs the Lord to allow her to have a child. She promises that she will bring the child to the temple forever.

So she made a request. I do that.

She made a promise. I do that.

HANNAH'S VOICE

She kept her promise.

She kept her promise.

Did I do that?

When she kept her promise, she put her selfishness aside—she surrendered! She is a profound example of surrender to God. She teaches us to seek God, to be faithful to God, and to surrender to God.

SEEK GOD

Hannah sought God. Hannah prayed to the Lord about her concerns. She was diligent in her prayers. She was accused of being drunk and she denied the accusation and persisted to pray.

When we seek God, we do not have permission to quit or ask without faith. When you ask God for something, you are to ask with TOTAL FAITH. Not the way you ask now, when you ask without hope or faith or belief or love for what God can do.

We lack total faith. We fail to exercise even 'relative faith.' Relative faith is when you use the faith and testimony of others who have received what they have asked of God. Relative faith should boost your personal faith. The use of relative faith is temporary—not a permanent solution to your lack of full-time faith.

We need to look at the faith of others so to insure that we have our own faith. Sometimes we need to know what faith looks like. We need to hear from others about the length of their season so that you can stop begging God as if He is not working and that He is not listening.

POWERFUL LESSONS IN PRAYER

There are debates about authentic faith versus borrowed faith. While I do not have a deep theological study or evidence, I will state that God uses the story and faith of others to establish, build and restore the faith of those of us with wavering, unsettled, and unstable faith. God reassures us that He has not ever disappointed us.

Hannah seeks God through prayer and not one could deter her from prayer. Hannah was not moved by the criticism she was receiving from even Eli, the priest.

When we consider Hannah's behavior we must be honest about our attitude about Hannah. We still criticize 'Hannah' today when we see others going through something or worship or their prayers. Hannah sought God through prayer—prayers that she shares as an example and a testimony of God's power and His plan. Seeking God is a daily, moment by moment, 24-7, pursuit via prayer, study and meditation.

We do not have the right or the time to criticize 'Hannah' because we need to imitate Hannah. We need to <u>be</u> Hannah. We need to seek God like Hannah has. For the reasons that Hannah does. For the length of time that Hannah did. So that we wait on the results that God will provide in His timing. God replied with an answer which only God can provide.

Seeking God diligently is the first step to surrender. Hannah recognized who is in controls. For all of us narcissists, raise your hand if you do not check with God first about things which ails you. As a control freak, the first person we consider is ourselves. We do not check with God first. The first step to surrender is to seek God first. FIRST. Not after all of your personal remedies, schemes or various activities. God is to be sought first.

HANNAH'S VOICE

Hannah seeks God. She does not quit when He does not answer her within 24 hours, 24 days or even 24 months.

Hannah is faithful.

FAITH IN GOD

Faith is beautiful when done faithfully. Faith is full-time. Faith is not faith if you take any breaks. God does not excuse you if you make an excuse of why you are not faithful. There is absolutely no acceptable reason: Hebrews 11:6 reads, "and without faith, it is impossible to please God, because anyone who comes to Him must believe that He exists and that He rewards those who earnestly seek Him."

Hannah demonstrates faith in God because she is persuaded to stop praying, when she is not convinced to give up the desire of her heart, and when she does not quit serving God with her whole heart.

Faith requires that we do two things: one, we do not discourage others from the desires of their heart nor the pursuit of God; and two, that we do not let others deter us from the desires of our hearts and the pursuit of God.

Hannah's husband almost made this category. His questions were 'wasn't he enough' and 'did she really need a child to be made whole.' That is what gives the devil a foothold. This is what causes doubt. This is what causes people to question God and consider what others have to say in conflict with God and His word.

Please be sure that you are not the person that does that to another person. As Christians, we are accountable to uphold the word of God with each other. This is possibly the hardest part of being a Christian—helping others to survive our lives, our mountains, our valleys, and our storms.

Faith is not optional. Faith is required as a Christian. Faith is to God as love is to us, as for relationships and what is expected. If you intend to please the person you are in a relationship with, love is required. In a relationship with God, faith is required. Have you ever considered that we do not get what we ask for because we do not ask with belief? Do we ask half-heartedly? Do we ask with doubt? Do we ask with fear? Do we ask with a haughty attitude? Do we ask without humility? Do we ask based on the last no God rendered?

These may be hindering us from being blessed with our desires. We want our desires on our time schedule. Do we ask with a time demand and deadline? Do you allow your children or family to ask you for something and they stop you from what you are doing so that they can receive it right now? We may need to consider that when we approach God to pray. Our timing and God's timing are at a significant mismatch and those times will be forever out of sync until we surrender with FAITH the way Hannah teaches us.

How does God define faith? How does God measure our faith? Who does God give us as examples of faith? What happens when we fail God due to a lack of faith? How do we reach the faith God expects of us? Faith and lack of faith is like yes and no—there is no in between, no gray area.

God defines faith as "faith is the substance of things hoped for and the evidence of things not seen." Hebrews 11:1 KJV. God defines faith as what we do in response or preparation for what we do not know or see. God defines faith as belief, without question, doubt or fear. God measures our faith based on our actions. Are our actions faithful? Or, are they the opposite, which are doubt, fear and question. Do we really believe in God? Do we follow God without disbelief? Are we present and doubtful? Are we Christian but we want to see what God does for someone else first before we believe? Are you still faithful when others suggest you quit? Do you still believe when others challenge you

HANNAH'S VOICE

about God and His responsiveness? Do you deny God? In good times and times of despair?

The list that God gives as examples of faith in Hebrews 11 is quite profound. God mentions Abel, Enoch, Noah, Abraham, Isaac, Jacob, Sarah, Joseph, Moses, Red Sea Survivors, Jericho army, Rahab, Gideon, Barak, Samson, Jephthah, David, Samuel, unnamed prophets, and others who were not named.

I would like to add Hannah, Ruth, Job, Mary, Joseph, Elizabeth, Zechariah, and Jesus. Can you be added to the examples of faith? I want to be added. I want to be an example of faith for myself and others because God has done exceedingly, abundantly, more than I could ever ask or think. Out of faith, I keep writing books. Out of faith, I keep teaching. Because of faith, I am waiting on God's answer to my prayers, questions, and concerns. I serve Him in spite of feeling lost and abandoned. I feel like Job often but I will not let anyone deter me from serving God. God is enough. Who among you is faithful? How are you measuring their faith? How are you measuring your faith? What causes you to abandon your faith? How long will God tolerate your lack of faith?

Cain did not have faith but Abel did so Cain was jealous and killed Abel. What happens when we are without faith? What does God do? Sometimes He gives our promises to someone else. Solomon built the temple David was supposed to build. I do not want my promises to be given to someone else. I want everything I want and everything God has for me as well. Greedy? Selfish? Not really. Let us understand that God wants His will to be done. God wants to give us the desires of our heart. Our desires have a cost: obedience and SURRENDER.

Faith is required! Faith requires a specific type of SURRENDER: immediate surrender, unconditional surrender and a trusting surrender. These three characteristics create TOTAL surrender.

POWERFUL LESSONS IN PRAYER

SURRENDER TO GOD

One of the most profound acts is when Hannah confesses her heart to Eli. At the end of verse 10 of this chapter, Hannah is weeping bitterly. In verse 11, she vows to God a most profound vow, a promise that if God granted her a son, then she would give that son to the Lord for all the days of his life and no razor would ever be used on his head.

In verse 12, she continues praying and while she is praying, Eli interrupts her. When most of us would have lied or avoided the questions altogether, Hannah shocked the world, or maybe just me, when Hannah stated, "I am woman who is deeply troubled. I was pouring out my soul to the Lord. I have been praying here out of my great anguish and grief."

Surrender to God means telling your whole true story—not some 'modified, make you look better, trying to hide your obvious pain beneath hair and makeup (whether yours naturally or purchased), you can't even remember the story you told' version of the truth you tell because you cannot hear your own truth out loud.

Hannah teaches surrender by praying authentically to God. Not that superficial prayer that we pray when we are desperate but not humble or even remotely close to being aligned to God, much less His will. We should consider carefully the prayers we pray and how God receives those prayers.

Hannah did not get angry or disrespectful with Eli. She answered him not expecting anything from him. She defended her prayers and she did not ever consider that Eli would pray in agreement with her as he did in verse 17.

Hannah did not keep her struggle a secret—she shared immediately. She did not argue about her situation and circumstances.

HANNAH'S VOICE

One of the greatest compliments I have ever received, and simultaneously the most intimidating characteristic about me for others, is my authenticity. When a fellow board member said that I was the most authentic person he knew, I was speechless and overwhelmed. I was certainly complimented. At the same time, I realized that his admiration was genuine but sometimes the authentic reputation of my words, thoughts, and deeds put people in an uncomfortable position but one where they were drawn to me, or that I have the influence I need for career and political influence and success.

Can you be authentic with God and others about God? Will your authenticity lead others to Christ? Can you share your actual, unedited story with others? With God? Can you be authentic without shame? Guilt? Disgust? Disdain for yourself or your story?

God is waiting on us to be authentic. God is waiting for us to share what our issues are, our prayers overall, the outcome God has provided, and when we are victorious. God gave us a testimony in order to share it with others. Our job as a Christian is to move others closer to God because of what we experience.

Surrendering to God is a sign of strength and courage, wisdom and humility, character and love.

Surrender communicates that we love God. Surrender means that we share our inner most thoughts without withholding the horrible thought which proceeded the special part that took place. Surrender means that you share with others so that they may pray with confidence and without hesitation.

Surrender is giving over what belongs to God to God. Sometimes we think that we are surrendering. The truth of the matter is that if you are surrendering, then you have never been 100% surrendered. You are trying to do something that you are uncertain that you want to achieve. When we actually surrender, there is a different behavior we possess. Surrender means that God is in control all of the time, under all circumstances, and in all situations.

What does surrender cost you? What does your lack of surrender cost God? When do you have your surrender scheduled? Who will benefit from your surrender? How do we give ourselves over to God and never take us back?

Surrender is not easy. It involves release of control. It means to release the control over something you did not invent, did not originate and did not design or create the future of. It means to release the control of yourself to your Creator. We have been seduced by the perils of power for so long and been in pursuit of power for so long that we think we are really in control of ourselves. God allows us to participate in our lives but we BELONG to God. God should be able to control us but we withhold ourselves from Him very often—almost all of the time.

We are not talking about surrender to a person because they are your parent, spouse, friend or boss. I am boldly suggesting that you remember that surrendering to our Creator is the BEST option! We are talking about God—the Creator, the Deliverer, the Savior, the Advocate, the Confidant, the Comforter, the Father, and so much more.

We are talking about the Man who created you (Genesis 1:26-27) and knew you before you were formed in your mother's womb (Jeremiah 1:5) and the Man who has plans for you to prosper you and not to harm (Jeremiah 29:11) and the Man who loves you unconditionally (John 3:16).

What is the reason you cannot surrender to God? Why should you surrender? Why should you not surrender? When will you surrender? Under what circumstances will you finally surrender? Why did Hannah surrender?

HANNAH'S VOICE

I believe Hannah surrendered because she was always surrendered. She knew her place with God. She really knew that she was aligned with God and her role with God. She surrendered when she could have misbehaved. She could have said things to Peninnah that could have caused her to need to seek God's forgiveness. She maintained her grace with God through her prayer life. Something we often neglect.

Surrender means giving God back the you which belongs to Him, without reservation, or complaint, or concern.

Most of us make decisions by the 'pro—versus—con' approach so make that list if you must as you consider surrendering to God. Hannah did not make that list but she did find the benefits profoundly outstanding.

Seek God.

Faithful to God.

Surrender to God.

Hannah did it, so can we.

Amen.

POWERFUL LESSONS IN PRAYER

HANNAH TEACHES SERVICE TO GOD

1 Samuel 1:18-20

[18] She said, "May your servant find favor in your eyes." Then she went her way and ate something, and her face was no longer downcast.

[19] Early the next morning they arose and worshiped before the LORD and then went back to their home at Ramah. Elkanah made love to his wife Hannah, and the LORD remembered her. [20] So in the course of time Hannah became pregnant and gave birth to a son. She named him Samuel, saying, "Because I asked the LORD for him."

SERMON

Service is defined by dictionary.com as an act of helpful activity. Service has 37 definitions, was used in 3 parts of speech, and as an idiom. "To do something for someone or an entity."

Hannah opens verse 18 with 'servant' as she refers to herself. Servant is a significant name because she has given herself to the service to God. This is not normal; she is unique. In verse 16, she declares to Eli that she is a servant of God through Eli. She uses the pronoun you to suggest possession of her and her servitude.

There are characteristics of a servant that she demonstrates that we need to take note of and considering mimicking her because she is such a great example.

HANNAH'S VOICE

ANNOUNCEMENT

In verses 16 and 18, Hannah announces that she is a servant. This declaration is significant because she recognizes that God is her Lord. She needs God and she seeks Him diligently.

Servant indicates that she has submitted herself to the work of God and to the people of God. In her prayers, she is humble and she is meek. She is committed to God, which she demonstrates in her prayers and her actions and her attitude and her humility.

Servant denotes that she exposed her heart and her truest feelings. Servant is giving our issues to God and submitting them to God for Him to handle. The announcement is a choice. She chose to announce her servitude. She could have chosen otherwise. She chose to obey God and declare that she is a servant. Servitude costs. Hannah did not have the benefit of Luke 9:23 but she certainly understood what Jesus meant when He said, "Whoever wants to be My disciple must deny themselves and take up their cross daily and follow me."

When she declared herself a servant, she acknowledged God's calling on her life. She graciously accepted that all on her life. She is not average. She is unique. She does not question her calling. She does not whine. She prays. She promises continued service. She asks for something that she will never possess! A request and trade some of us will never make! We make promises to God that we will never keep. However by example, Hannah let us know that she is committed to a God she believes for all things and is dedicated to whatever God's will is.

This lesson is one of the ultimate lessons in Christian maturity.

Then she had the audacity to offer her not yet conceived child to serve the Lord as well. That is faith and belief and service to God! She brings the statement 'as for me **and** my house, we will serve the Lord' to a new level! I was not bold enough to promise my children to God in the same manner and to keep my word!

Any announcement to serve God will bring you some attention. Elkanah's other wife was part of that attention. She behaved horribly. She teased her and berated her. She flaunted her children before Hannah. Hannah was not reported to respond, but certainly based on what God did, she never responded. Further, she never let those comments and that attitude deter her from believing that God is real and that He will do what He wants no matter what others have to say.

When you make an announcement to serve Christ, you can expect some resistance. You can expect some 'haters.' You can expect some obstacles. You can expect some challenges. How you choose to address those challenges will make the difference to God.

ACTION

Early the next morning they arose and worshipped before the Lord and then went back to their home at Ramah.

Actions speak louder than words. More is caught than is taught. Those are two clichés and they are true. Think about how you learn. How do you retain information? Well if you are honest, we learn by observation most of the time. We retain information through repetition. All of that is action.

Worship is a verb. To worship is go before the Lord and give God your undivided attention. Hannah took action: she worshipped. She did not whine. Nor did she pout. She did not return insult for insult. She did not even question her husband. She was diligent in her pursuit of God through prayer and worship.

HANNAH'S VOICE

She took action! She did not seek idols. She did not turn to her 'go-to's.' She turned to the Master.

Action. God honors actions which honor Him. What we learn from Hannah is that we cannot whine about what we do not have. Further, Hannah also shares with us that we cannot stop serving God, especially when we do not have what we desire.

Activities that honor God: prayer, worship, praise, grace, forgiveness, love and the other fruits of the spirit.

How can we give God the best of us under our worst conditions? When most of us want to quit, we need to want to persevere through our situations with our hand in God's hand, rather than with our arms folded. That requires maturity and FAITH. The best way to exhibit our faith to God is to believe Him and wait for Him while He is working on our behalf and to deliver what He has for you.

What are my actions which show God that I am faithful? By His definition?

ALIGNED

After the announcement and the actions, Hannah is aligned with God and God's will. Aligned to God's will means that we understand that our desires and God's will may differ so we are prepared to surrender to God's will.

Aligned means no excuses for God's decisions. Aligned means no exceptions from what God chooses. Aligned means that we do not complain and we try to see the situation God's way.

POWERFUL LESSONS IN PRAYER

There is the testimony that you have that clearly and boldly states that God should have the last say in all matters. What is yours? Hannah's is that she left the situation is God's hands—completely.

I have several testimonies where once I surrendered and God was in control, I was able to see what God had done, why His decision was best, and why I was wrong for interfering in the matter in the first place.

Hannah does not question God. She aligns to His will. She submits her petition and then waits—actively. It is easier to surrender if you are not worrying and fretting. Peace is given through supplication. God is peace and love and grace and salvation . . . if we submit, surrender, and are still.

Exodus 14:14 reads "He will fight your battles if you just be still."

I have to be reminded to be aligned with God. I am constantly trying to help God, supersede God, step around God and supplant God. None of that is my job. God is God and God alone. He does not need any help or supervision. He does not need my suggestions or solutions. Because He is God. God has a plan. God has THE plan!

God used Hannah for **the plan** because she was aligned with God. God cannot use us when we insist on being out of His will, or question His plan, or consider His plans as optional. Some of this will seem repetitive, however, it is important to repeat it for emphasis and importance.

ACCOUNTABLE

We are accountable to God. Hannah highlights why that being accountable to God is important. Hannah did not forget what she promised God. She did not

HANNAH'S VOICE

forget the deal she made with God. She did not cheapen God's fulfillment of her desire, and ultimately His will.

When we are accountable to God, He can trust us with major parts of His will. God trusted Hannah to birth after a series of tests of her commitment to Him.

God could only trust certain women to birth the men He called in His kingdom. Hannah was called, thus trusted, to birth Samuel.

When we consider how important Samuel is to God and to the history of the Church, we need to understand why our behavior determines what God can use us to do. If we peek into Samuel's future, then we will see that God called for Samuel (1 Samuel 3), Samuel preached (1 Samuel 4), God afflicted those who possessed the Ark of God's covenant since it was stolen (1 Samuel 5 & 6), Samuel intercedes (1 Samuel 7), Samuel was a servant to God and eventually stood to appoint a king over all of Israel (1 Samuel 8), Samuel anoints Saul (1 Samuel 9), Samuel rebukes Saul, the king (1 Samuel 13), and Samuel anoints David (1 Samuel 16). Considering what we know about these brief chapters, we can understand why God needed the mother of Samuel to be serious about her walk and commitment to God.

Hannah is gifted with more children. Her initial job is similar to a few others: Eve, Sarah, Mary, Elizabeth, Bathsheba, and others we have not mentioned.

Hannah's accountability stretched far. What if she had changed her mind about giving Samuel back to the Lord? What if she had 'forgotten' her promise? What if she had not kept her word? All of that is considered spiritual character. God has to be able to trust us with our assignments. Hannah proved to God that she was able to carry out the assigned responsibilities.

God listened to her prayers. God watched her behavior with others. God watched how Elkanah treated her. God watched how Eli treated her. God watched all of the important factors so that He could carry out His will. When God was completely satisfied with the total picture, then God blessed her by opening her womb.

At three years old, Samuel worshipped before the Lord under the supervision of Eli. I am sure that at some point their wonderful story was shared. Because the family traveled to the temple each year, Hannah saw her son each year.

Accountable to God yields blessings. Accountability means that we consider that God's will supersedes our desires. Accountability means that when we do not get our way, we do not moan, groan, whine, or complain.

Accountability means that we share our testimony with others as necessary. That testimony will be criticized and scrutinized. You may be ridiculed or teased but mostly you will be blessed by the God who orchestrated the entire process.

After an announcement, actions, alignment, and accountability, Hannah blesses us so that we can bless others. Hannah does not have to be alive for her life to judge ours, nor for it to be a tool to model after as improvement to our own. In all of what she does, she taught us to serve God: wholly, completely, sacrificially, and without reward if that was God's will.

God's will is too profound for us to be selected haphazardly. God needs to know that nothing and no one can intercept us from Him and His will. Not at any time. Not for any reason.

Hannah's service allowed her to be in God's will.

Amen.

HANNAH'S VOICE

POWERFUL LESSONS IN PRAYER

HANNAH TEACHES OBEDIENCE TO GOD

1 Samuel 1:21-28

Hannah Dedicates Samuel

[21] When her husband Elkanah went up with all his family to offer the annual sacrifice to the LORD and to fulfill his vow, [22] Hannah did not go. She said to her husband, "After the boy is weaned, I will take him and present him before the LORD, and he will live there always."

[23] "Do what seems best to you," her husband Elkanah told her. "Stay here until you have weaned him; only may the LORD make good his word." So the woman stayed at home and nursed her son until she had weaned him.

[24] After he was weaned, she took the boy with her, young as he was, along with a three-year-old bull, an ephah of flour and a skin of wine, and brought him to the house of the LORD at Shiloh. [25] When the bull had been sacrificed, they brought the boy to Eli, [26] and she said to him, "Pardon me, my lord. As surely as you live, I am the woman who stood here beside you praying to the LORD. [27] I prayed for this child, and the LORD has granted me what I asked of him. [28] So now I give him to the LORD. For his whole life he will be given over to the LORD." And he worshiped the LORD there.

SERMON

As a mom, I consider pregnancy a gift from God. The most important part of that gift is the stewardship. God gives us children to parent for His purposes. God has a plan and when He chooses us to participate in His plan, obedience is required.

HANNAH'S VOICE

Naming our children is equally as important. When I named my son, I was going to match our initials, but God said otherwise. God spoke to me and said, 'Name this boy Nehemiah.' I did not have medical confirmation that I was having a son but his name would be Nehemiah.

I am not amazed that God would name His child while in my womb because God had done that several times already. I was not new nor special.

God did this with Hannah as well. God selected Hannah to birth Samuel because of several reasons, many of which we may never know, but one thing is for sure, God trusted Hannah. Hannah was obedient. Hannah teaches obedience to God.

SACRIFICE

Make no mistake, Hannah had been on a long, lonely and arduous journey. She had wanted a child for years, but had been barren. In the previous scriptures, her story is outlined on the request that she makes of God. Based on her request that she makes of god. Based on her request, she made a promise as well.

Hannah has been on this long journey and she was rewarded with a son, Samuel. At the culmination of this journey, she has to take Samuel to the church. She is no longer going to raise him at her home.

Hannah sacrifices Samuel. She gives Samuel to God in such a manner that she demonstrates an obedience which is simply unprecedented. Hannah did something that so many of us don't do: she keeps her word.

Hannah teaches obedience with her sacrifice. Hannah could have 'forgotten' her 'deal.' Don't you think that she wanted to change her mind? But her heart was set on understanding God for His grace on her life. Hannah shows us that her sacrifice via obedience is pleasing to God. Because she pleased God, Hannah reaped several children after Samuel. God rewarded Hannah because He trusted Hannah.

Hannah just wanted to know that the Lord would bless her because she asked, because she was faithful and because her motives were pure. God does not always reward our sacrifice or obedience in the same manner. Hannah happened to be the recipient of an unexpected series of blessings.

Sacrifice is trusting God. When we sacrifice our desires, we demonstrate our trust of our God. We then exercise our duties as a disciple—we denied ourselves for what God wants. Sometimes our sacrifice seems more than what others have to sacrifice before they are blessed. Sometimes the sacrifice seems bigger than other sacrifices. Remember at all times, God is in control. The difference between voluntary and involuntary sacrifice is the matters before God which pertain to us. There are situations when God causes you to give up something that was mistakenly placed in priority before God. This involuntary sacrifice is designed to remind us that God is a jealous God and will not compete with other people or events or situations or preferences.

Abraham was called to sacrifice Isaac, the son God promised Abraham. So it stands to reason that Abraham was disappointed in this request. But Abraham obeyed and complied and took Isaac to the place God prepared for him to sacrifice the gift. God wanted to see what Abraham would do—will you trust Me, Abraham? But just when Abraham was ready to actually kill the boy, God said, "I see what you will do for Me; keep the gift I gave you. Instead there is a ram in the bush that I will accept in place of Isaac because I am firm that NOTHING stands between Us."

As you consider this story, please reflect on times when you failed God's test of trust. You promised that if God did what you requested then you would do something. The problem is that God did what you asked but you failed on your part. You rationalized that it would be okay. You bargained with yourself. You convinced yourself that God did not want what you offered. But you were wrong! You offered God a sacrifice but reneged—you defaulted on the deal! This is why we should not make deals with God.

I made a deal with God once and I held up my part. One of the reasons was I was scared that God would take my car back. When we love God, we sacrifice. We have to consider what God wants from us. We have to understand that God shares us with everything else and we need to measure our sacrifice, and really determine what we really give God. Sacrifice is when we give to God what we want to keep for ourselves. Sacrifice is giving when we do not want to. Sacrifice is giving when we do not know when we will have 'this' again. Sacrifice is giving when you do not know if the resources will ever be restored. Sacrifice hurts often. Sacrifice causes deep reflection of ourselves and our situation. Hannah demonstrates her ultimate sacrifice by giving the very gift she craved but she gave Samuel to the Lord anyway.

What do you need to sacrifice for a better relationship with God? What will God do for you if you give up the very thing you stake your reputation on? What will God do for you if you give up the things which distract you from God? What will God do for you if you passed the test of sacrifice and surrender?

SHOW

Sacrifice requires showing God that you are serious about your relationship. Part of showing this sacrifice is for others to see what God does within us.

When we have sacrificed for God, we can show up for God. Give God what you promised Him, when you bargained with God.

POWERFUL LESSONS IN PRAYER

Give God what you owe Him. In the physical world, when you make a deal—a debt—you pay that debt or you pay the consequences. Let us consider a what if! What if God changed His mind? What if He had never brought the Israelites out of Egypt? What if He had not given Noah the ark? What if Hannah had not prayed? Would there have been a Samuel? What if God had not made David the King?

What if God decided that we were not forgivable and we were not worth Jesus' death? What if Jesus decided to get down off of the cross? What if He had negotiated with God for a different path?

What if God ignored His plan for us, although we were in the plan before the beginning of the world?

What if God changed His mind because we lied to Him?

I love Hannah's story because Hannah kept focus on God. She never quit pursuing the heart of God. She never quit pursuing the heart of God for her needs. She pursued Him with faith the He would provide. She never even considered changing her mind. When God blessed her with Samuel, she weaned him, took him to the temple, and never looked back!

Don't ever promise God something without knowing that you will actually follow up and keep your promise, and that you can expect some consequences for not keeping your word and otherwise bargaining with God.

When you decide to bargain or negotiate with God, be sure that you understand the implications of that decision.

Be who you say you are! You are a creation of God but you act fake and lie to God. This is an act of disobedience. This disobedience demonstrates your lack of love for God. Just think if we were obedient, what He created, what would God do in response to that?

Be who you are supposed to be—all the time! Show God, then you will show yourself—proving that you are not a total heathen.

SHARE

Hannah had a long journey with barrenness. She wanted a child for a very long time. She begged God for a child—one she promised to give back. Hannah did that: she gave back Samuel to God by sending Samuel to Eli to raise and groom and whatever else God would like for Samuel to do.

Hannah shared with others what God did and what God will do and what she did to serve God.

Hannah served God from the first request to the delivery of Samuel to the temple. Hannah was forth coming in her quest and her method of seeking God. Hannah was transparent about her desires for a son. She was transparent about her hurt and pain. She was transparent about her survival methods. She was honest and authentic and transparent about her situation and circumstances and the condition of her heart.

I can assure you that most of us are not anything like Hannah. On the other hand, we lie, we hide, we sulk, and we harbor ill will. We wear a mask. We do not share what we desire from God. We do not share because if God does not answer our prayer according to our desire, we will be ashamed and we may be mocked by those who are the audience to our lives. We do not want to share with them because we are afraid that God will say no. This no will lead to the

POWERFUL LESSONS IN PRAYER

doubt that is already fostering within you and any addition to that doubt will lead to a complete dismemberment of the teaspoon of faith you are barely using.

We are all in that place. We are scarred so we are scared to be transparent. We are not able to share without wondering if the audience will hurt us . . . again. Our ability to share is stifled by our past as well as our personal insecurities. Both of these can only be overcome by following Hannah's example.

Hannah teaches us to present what we desire before the Lord, unashamedly, unapologetically, and immediately. When she stopped hiding her needs and exposed her heart in public while praying to God, she made God first and most important. She could not help herself any better than sharing with Eli her needs. She was not afraid to pray publicly, not to mention, when Eli accused her being drunk, she immediately shared her situation. Eli did not have to beg her.

Hannah teaches us how to put God first. Hannah prays in faith, fully believing God to deliver.

She wants the baby but she wants God's favor more. She teaches us to share our desires with God. She teaches us to share with our spiritual leaders our desires and needs. Hannah teaches us to expose yourself so that others do not have the opportunity to do anything that prevents you from serving the God that loves you, protects you, and keeps you from failing and falling.

Hannah understood what God wants and expects: our undivided attention. Instead of allowing for barrenness to separate her from God, she committed her barrenness and her life to God in an outlandish and outrageous and extravagant manner. When she totally surrendered to God, she gained a promise and she demonstrated an unbelievable obedience.

Hannah raised the standard and the bar in prayer and in life. This step is one most of us are too weak to consider. For us to boldly pray and give over our

HANNAH'S VOICE

burdens to God is the start of the relationship with God which He has ordained each of us.

Sharing is not normal for us, but we must so that God can be glorified.

Share what God is doing, what God has done, and what God is able to do.

Share openly.

Share boldly.

Share outlandishly.

Share outrageously.

Share extravagantly.

When you are sharing your testimony, be honest, be transparent, be humble, and be bold.

God deserves all of that!

Amen.

HANNAH TEACHES HOW TO SEEK GOD WITH ZEAL

1 Samuel 2:1-2

¹ Then Hannah prayed and said:

"My heart rejoices in the LORD;
   in the LORD my horn is lifted high.
My mouth boasts over my enemies,
   for I delight in your deliverance.

² "There is no one holy like the LORD;
   there is no one besides you;
   there is no Rock like our God.

SERMON

Hannah rejoices in the Lord because of what God has done. She prays with a mouth and heart full of praise! She is not shy or ashamed about praying before the Lord, nor about praying aloud where others can hear but not for show.

Hannah teaches us how to seek God with zeal. For the purpose of background, Hannah has been barren for the duration of her marriage. She pursued God diligently a few years before this text was written. She prayed. God answered her prayer in an abounding manner—God said yes. God gave her Samuel. Because she promised Samuel to God, she took Samuel to the temple and left him there.

This text follows her leaving Samuel there. She comes home and openly rejoices.

HANNAH'S VOICE

She comes home and openly rejoices. With what we know and have experienced with Hannah, she forces us to answer some questions of ourselves.

One such question is 'are we joyful while we wait on God to answer or when God says no? Do we immediately rejoice and give God glory? Do we share God's goodness when God delivers what we request?

Are we keepers of our promises?

Do we see what God sees when we ask and receive, seek and find?

Do we consistently appreciate God the way He deserves?

Are we ashamed to pray, serve, evangelize, and use our gifts but not ashamed to drive that car?

Well with a zeal that is worthy of sharing, let us walk through the text to see Hannah lessons.

OVERWHELMED HEART

Based on the brief, yet powerful recount of Hannah's life, I believe that Hannah would have prayed a remarkable similar prayer even if God had not given her a child. Hannah exhibited an unbelievable faith. Hannah exercised a faith that pleased God. She prayed with the zeal from an overwhelmed spirit. This would lead to an overwhelmed heart.

Gage defines an overwhelmed heart as one which experiences awesome and disappointment with the same level of faith, attitude and love for God. An overwhelmed heart cannot be deterred from God; regardless of the nature of the day or circumstances or events or situations. An overwhelmed heart makes no excuses. An overwhelmed heart does not retain or harbor ill will towards others. An overwhelmed heart demonstrates love regardless of the situation.

An overwhelmed heart does not have time for malice; deceit or gossip.

An overwhelmed heart is overwhelmed with God. An overwhelmed heart is concerned with what God says, God's word, God's will, God's work, and God's love.

When we consider the definition of overwhelmed, it does not have a positive connotation. Quite the opposite actually. However, if we use the definition "to load, heap, treat, or address with an overpowering or excessive amount of anything," then we could actually address the matter of an overwhelmed heart for God. God's love is overwhelming, but we push it aside and take a portion of it for ourselves but we do not deserve His love. If we allowed, via surrender, God's love to completely cover us and to complete us, then we would have an overwhelmed heart. We would then behave like God loves us.

Hannah demonstrated an overwhelmed heart because she was obedient. Hannah did not have the benefit of Hannah. She had to follow God. We have the benefit of her story so we can use it for our own lives as an example. She did not have the benefit of the entire Bible, while we have the entire Bible, we have it in several hundred translations, along with commentaries, dictionaries, and several other resources. Even with all of that, we have a partitioned heart! We limit God's access to our whole heart—the heart God gave us. God intended for our hearts to be overwhelmed.

God's work in a hardened, partitioned heart is different from that of an overwhelmed heart. God has to do extra work in the hardened heart. We look at Hannah to understand our behavior and what it should be when we desire what

HANNAH'S VOICE

we do not have and we are waiting on God to answer us. Hannah demonstrates what we need to do while we wait and even if we get denied the request.

Hannah demonstrates what we should do in all situations, especially if we are not hearing from God on our timing. How do we get to an overwhelmed heart?

It is a great place to be.

We develop an overwhelmed heart by surrendering our issues to God. We confess our heart condition to God. When we confess all that we are and all that we want to God, then you are on your way to an overwhelmed heart.

We submit to the will of God when our hearts are overwhelmed. The will of God in non-negotiable, non-debatable, and non-permissive—it does not require our consent. Giving over our desires to God and even giving up our desires to serve God is an overwhelmed heart.

Ask God to show you where you can have an overwhelmed heart. God will show you how to have an overwhelmed heart. God will show you how to demonstrate an overwhelmed heart to others. God will put your overwhelmed heart to the test. God will put your overwhelmed heart to use. God will help you teach others like Hannah teaches us to use your overwhelmed heart.

OUTLANDISH SPIRIT

An overwhelmed heart escorts in an outlandish spirit. The word outlandish has never been contextually meant anything positive. It has been used in context to mean something horribly ridiculous and has no merit at all. However dictionary.com states that outlandish is "freakishly or grotesquely strange or odd, as in appearance, dress, objects, ideas, or practices; bizarre."

POWERFUL LESSONS IN PRAYER

When I first used the word outlandish, a young lady brought to my attention that it had never been positive. Upon reading the definition, I understood her point however, I feel that we can use outlandish to pursue positivity and be intentional about serving God.

Let us examine an outlandish spirit.

Outlandish spirit is a spirit committed to God—simply sold out for God.

Hannah has an outlandish spirit. She does something which indicates that God has her full and undivided attention.

Verse one states that her heart rejoices in the Lord. That is a bold statement! Can we say that? Are we WHYDFML worshippers of God? Oh, the acronym got you? **'What Have You Done For Me Lately'** is what triggers our worship and praise.

When I consider how bold Hannah has been this entire time, I shrink. She stirs within me the need to surrender completely to God. Well you may be thinking, 'Reverend Onedia, when are you not totally surrendered to God?' Well, I am glad you asked. I am not totally surrendered when I do not pray daily and when I miss the opportunity to return my burdens to God. I do this when I doubt God's ability to overcome my obstacles or when I forget that God's will always prevails. I do this when I want my way without the benefit of the full picture, which God has completely. I really do this when I intentionally sin against God; when I sin because I am having a bad day, horrible week, or feel abandoned, instead of going to God and leaving <u>all</u> <u>of</u> <u>that</u> <u>at</u> <u>His</u> <u>feet</u>.

Well Hannah and I share a God that you and I can go to just like Hannah did. And she kneeled before the Father declaring her love, admiration, and respect for all that God is. She used words like delight, rejoice, lifted, and deliverance. These are bold and outlandish words and statements by which the Lord

HANNAH'S VOICE

responds. God accepts her declaration and her adoration and her appreciation and support because He trusts her and all of her behavior was consistent with her words and her thoughts. This is an outlandish spirit. God recognizes the authentic attitude and the humble disposition. God sees the meekness and receives the genuine praise. All because of her outlandish spirit.

What if you are like me and sometimes your spirit is less than outlandish? What if you have never had an outlandish spirit? Here is what Hannah teaches us.

Surrender to God—everything we are, we have, we need, we want, how we feel, what we think, love we have, indifference we possess, hatred we clutch, and unconfessed and repeated sins that we commit.

Hannah teaches that we are to bear our soul to God. We are to praise God more than the people we love and stars we admire. Hannah helps us abandon pride. Hannah teaches how valuable admiration is.

Her spirit unfolds before the Lord in a manner which should make you blush and give Hannah and God your full attention. Her focus on God is to be modeled as well. She gives God the undivided attention of her heart, mind and spirit.

When God delivered her, she immediately turned toward God.

ONLY GOD

Often we put ourselves and all of our accoutrements before God. We make God wait until we are settled and until we are ready to serve Him. We want God to accept the time and prayers and service we dole out to Him at our leisure, but we want God to intervene as soon as the doctor renders his diagnosis and as soon as we realize that our retirement savings has been lost and as soon as our child is sentenced to time in jail. We need to remember that God does not respond in kind.

We often do not understand how we make God last after everything. I know that seems extreme. You may try to argue that God is not actually last, but maybe third or fourth, but what we need to realize is that if God is not first then He is last. There is only one place for God: FIRST. God wants us to make God our choice. We need to make God first at all times, in all situations, for all seasons, because of all consequences, and to do so daily.

As Hannah rejoices to God, she dedicates herself to the God that she puts first. She remembered that God blessed her with a child, for whom she had prayed. As Hannah worships God, she tells God that no one is Holy like You, God. She says there is no rock like our God.

Hannah tells God that because she knows that God deserves this praise and worship. God is first to Hannah—before her husband AND the son that God gave her! If God was testing Hannah for the worth of her heart, Hannah passed that test with flying colors.

Hannah did not worship God for us—she worshipped God for herself. She demonstrated it to us because she was already doing for herself and God. She shares her testimony because God was pleased with her.

I am leery to share my testimony. I cannot tell everyone what I have been through because I require that you never use what has happened to me against me. That is the devil at work within another. If you use my testimony to try to sabotage my future, it is my belief that the devil holding onto you really tightly and has an urgent quest for your soul. If you cannot see God's hand and deliverance and cannot see how God will do the same for you, but instead tries to sabotage my future, I will pray for you. However, I see the devil on you and within you which is what is preventing you from seeking God with zeal.

Only God can deliver us from our sins and our troubles. Only God can deliver us from our personal places of destruction. Only God can pluck us from the hands of the enemy. Only God can offer our enemies as a footstool. Only God can cause our enemies to wonder why the trap they set for us is one used to cause them to fail. Only God can give you what you need when you need it on His time because He is God.

Stop questioning God.

Stop questioning God.

Stop the perfunctory talks with God.

They would be prayers except we sound like we are talking to someone other than God about our needs and issues and dreams and desires.

Stop meddling in God's business.

Stop avoiding serving God.

Stop reminding God of your inabilities.

Stop throwing tantrums.

Stop issuing ultimatums to God.

Stop acting like God does not hear you or that He is ignoring you.

Only God can take our mess and turn it into a message. One where Only God gets the glory, honor and well-deserved praise! Only God deserves the best of us. Only God will appreciate us and everything that we produce because we are His workmanship. Only God can address us at the depths of who we are.

Only God is the lifter of our heads. Our hearts. Our minds. Ourselves.

Hannah was a vessel to teach us to pursue and praise God with an outlandish and outrageous pursuit of God that proves that we love Him despite ourselves and because of our less than perfect lives.

When you forget why you exist or what God has done for you and what He uses you to do, review Hannah.

With an overwhelmed heart and an outlandish spirit, I will serve the Only God.

Amen.

HANNAH'S VOICE

POWERFUL LESSONS IN PRAYER

Hannah Prays Fervently

1 Samuel 2:3-5

³ "Do not keep talking so proudly
   or let your mouth speak such arrogance,
for the LORD is a God who knows,
   and by him deeds are weighed.
⁴ "The bows of the warriors are broken,
   but those who stumbled are armed with strength.
⁵ Those who were full hire themselves out for food,
   but those who were hungry are hungry no more.
She who was barren has borne seven children,
   but she who has had many sons pines away.

SERMON

Hannah prayed the prayer of thanks, courage, wisdom, knowledge, and encouragement. She discusses her own attitude, that of the other wife, Peninnah, and most of us. This is not someone else's story; this is yours and mine.

Between bitter, broken and barren, we have all experienced at least one of these feelings—often more than once. The lesson is how to avoid these having a long term effect on us. Hannah also shares what God does in response to our situations.

Bitter, broken and barren should cause us to rise to the next level. These three aspects should drive us to closer to God. These three feelings are designed by the enemy to drive you away from God.

HANNAH'S VOICE

BITTER

If you have ever been bitter, then you know that surviving bitterness requires skills. Bitterness can halt your joy and peace in an abominable way without reprieve. Bitterness can hold you hostage without your knowledge. Often you don't realize that you are in that place until it is revealed to you by way of spirit or person. One truth for certain is that we are never ready to hear it.

Bitterness has the power over the spirit like cancer has power over the body part it has invaded. Bitterness is cancerous and causes you to be cantankerous.

Bitterness is an offspring of pride. This pride is the start of bitterness because pride and arrogance fails. Bitterness develops when you do not receive what you believe that you deserve. Bitterness is not realized until rejection is repeated. Bitterness is evident when we consider that we have been forgotten and forsaken.

Bitterness, once seated and intertwined, chokes out your kindness, meekness, and peacefulness. Bitterness challenges your ability to love, your long-suffering, your thoughts, and your reasoning. Bitterness considers an end to your faithfulness, gentleness, self-control, and joy. Bitterness creates anger and hostility. Bitterness causes you to be less than lovable, friendly, faithful, and positive.

Bitterness could have captured Hannah but prayer saved her from bitterness and all of its accoutrements.

Hannah did also steer clear of the trap of pride, which many of us fall right into every time. We cannot let that trap us—neither pride nor bitterness.

Why do we allow bitterness control us? We are strong enough to pray through bitterness. Arrogance is over compensation.

POWERFUL LESSONS IN PRAYER

BROKEN

I am broken.

You are broken.

There have been situations which have pushed us and tested us. There have been some which have broken us. Or so we assumed.

When we say the vase is broken, we mean that it is in a lot of pieces—impossible to put back together in the same way and it will never be seen the same again. Even if you could get really close to perfect and it appears as if nothing happened, the story behind the previously broken, now repaired, vase will be told over and over again. Isn't that what we do?

We tell how we were broken. We tell how we were battered and all of the details which brought us to broken.

What we do not do share is how we were put back together. We neglect to share how God put us back together.

What does it take to be put back together? What did God do to put you back together? When you realize that God has blessed you and that God is putting you back together, what do you do?

Hannah shares what God has done, but more importantly, she praises God for what He has done. She shares that God overcomes all of our issues. She tells that God puts us back together in an amazing way—a way that we could not imagine or conceive.

Hannah testifies that God is a Fixer, a Healer. She says that God retrieves those who have stumbled and have restored them with strength.

HANNAH'S VOICE

God equipped His warriors with strength even though they have broken tools. God has equipped us beyond our knowledge. The visible and obvious tools are not the only tools we are equipped with. Our hidden tools may be better than we are able to comprehend.

Hannah shows us her inner strength. She shares her heart of prayer—the most powerful tool yet overall.

God equips us for the battles we are placed in. There is strength only accessible for that particular battle. Strength which causes you to ask yourself what happened and which will create within you a great spirit of overwhelm for the grace God has given you during this season of battle.

Broken can be repaired. Broken does not stop any action. Broken does not stop God's will. Broken can heal. Broken is a testimony. Remember in many cases broken happened but not many witnessed it. Further, broken occurred but it is not visible to the naked eye. Broken cannot be seen from the outside, but it exists and is on repair within the confines of the body, mind, and spirit. Keeping in mind that we are working to keep that brokenness out of the public view through our words, deeds, and actions.

Broken can be survived. Broken can be endured. Broken can be victorious.

Hannah was broken. We are broken and have been broken under different circumstances and situations. Hannah emerged victorious and she shared the gory details and she shared what God did.

She testifies through prayer that God has done something amazing in a not—so—ordinary way. When she prays, those who stumbled are armed with strength. She tells me that God retrieved and did not abandon, yet empowered the broken. She announces that there is hope for the broken, and healing is available. She reminds us that God knows our situation and our location—He knows just the state that we are in.

We needed that reminder because the broken without hope will forget all of that. It is hard to remember anything positive when you are broken.

When we praise God through our brokenness, we then take the focus off of our personal situation and focus on He who can heal, supply victory, and withstand all that we are in need of to survive as we prepare to be victorious.

BARREN

Physical barrenness is a reality for many women still today. They CRAVE a baby. Hannah teaches us that when God assigns us to a child, it is a responsibility, a calling.

Hannah seeks God for her concerns. Once God gifts her with Samuel, she prays with thanksgiving. This prayer of thanksgiving is joyful and rejoicing and grateful.

Hannah commits her heart, soul, and body to God. Hannah insists that He feeds those who are hungry. She remembers that He is the Source.

Hannah shares her rejoice for being blessed seven times over the barren issue. She also notes that when God is your only Source, your blessings have joy.

When Hannah says 'pines away,' she is referring to someone who is discontent, what they have and what they asked for seems insufficient. We need to consider that concept. What happens when you are not satisfied with what you have; you no longer see it as a blessing?

HANNAH'S VOICE

Let's review for a moment: the other wife taunts Hannah for not having children. Then Hannah has Samuel. She takes Samuel to the church in care of the priest. The other wife is now upset that her taunting turned into joy because Hannah and she are equal now. Did Peninah need something to hold over someone's head or rub into someone else's face in order to feel like a woman—a whole woman? That is gone so now what do you do? She is feeling awkward and less than special. She can no longer gloat about her 'blessings.'

Is that how we behave? Do we taunt people with what we have? Do we lord over them with our blessings and belongings? Do we tease them about what they do not have? Do we tease them with what we do have? Do we criticize them for who they are because they are not who we want them to be?

We do. We reject others but do not want to be rejected. We taunt people and tease them for not having what we have. We use others for what we need and when we are done, we discard them. We do all of those things but we should not. We would not want to be treated in that manner, and because of that, we should remember to not engage in that behavior.

Peace is a powerful experience. Hannah prays with such peace. She lives with that same peace. She prays with that same peace. She parents with that peace. She pursues God with that same peace. This peace in not earned or bought or borrowed. This peace is a gift, from God, which transcends our complete understanding. This means that even if I am peaceful in that manner, I may not be able to explain the fullness that God's peace provides. It is not as simple as how a roller coaster is built or operates. It is not as simple as washing your hands or picking up your cell phone. This place is powerful beyond measure. It is powerful beyond measure because it is from God.

POWERFUL LESSONS IN PRAYER

We need that peace because our souls are barren. We are not feeding our souls! WE neglect our spirits because of our busy-ness and we do not realize that we are neglecting the nucleus of who we are.

We need to insure that we are feeding our souls properly and regularly. When was the last time you read your Bible? Joined a study group? Attended Bible study? Prayed? Attended church? When it wasn't a holiday? These are all events which assist you to replenish your soul and nourish your spirit. This is quality time with God.

Keep in mind that we are fragile. We need God to help us to overcome our barrenness and rebuilding our spirituality is most importantly. We need to seek God for everything. We often do not.

God has overcome barrenness in your life before now. He showed up during that miscarriage and divorce. He showed up during your unemployment and your depression. God was there when your child got pregnant and when he nearly failed college. God was there when you thought your own life didn't have a purpose. God was there then you suffered through that physical pain and the surgery and the recovery and the healing. God was there then you had little and when you had plenty. God was there when you failed that major test. God was there then that test did not stop your career. God has been there when you have done it all.

God has a solution for your barrenness. God knows the path He established for you. God keeps you when you feel faint, want to faint, cannot wait to faint, and actually, do faint.

HANNAH TEACHES PRAYING FERVENTLY

God is the solution to your bitterness. God has the power to heal your brokenness. God is the solution to your brokenness. Hannah is no different from

HANNAH'S VOICE

us. We want God to bless us, and to solve our problems, and to give us the desires our hearts. We want to be healed from barrenness. In order for that to happen, we need to be obedient. God expects us to pray and study and fast and live orderly lives. There are times when we fail and when we succeed. There are times when we are remorseful and times when we are naughty; downright arrogant about our transgressions and behaviors. Hannah humbled herself. She showed a complete stranger her heart. She made a BOLD promise to God which she kept. She is an example of how God expects us to behave and submit ourselves to Him.

What are we praying for? What do you want God to do? Will you share what God has done for you authentically, genuinely, and remarkably? Will you share unashamedly? Will you share Him like you love Him—the way you expect Him to respond to you?

Will you serve God in an outrageous and outlandish manner? Will you thank Him for the opportunity to do all things? Will you keep the promises you make to Him?

Will you consider that God is the Creator and Jesus is the Redeemer and even when we fail, God has a way of brushing us off and putting out feet on solid ground such that we may remain standing for Him?

Let's walk away from the stronghold that our circumstances exercises over us. Let's give back the bitterness, brokenness, and barrenness that we have experienced so that we may have joy and strength and courage and deliverance.

No more bitterness.

No more brokenness.

No more barrenness.

In Jesus' name. Amen.

HANNAH'S VOICE

HANNAH GIVES SOUND ADVICE

1 Samuel 2:6-8

⁶ "The LORD brings death and makes alive;

   he brings down to the grave and raises up.

⁷ The LORD sends poverty and wealth;

   he humbles and he exalts.

⁸ He raises the poor from the dust

   and lifts the needy from the ash heap;

he seats them with princes

   and has them inherit a throne of honor.

"For the foundations of the earth are the LORD's;

   on them he has set the world.

SERMON

Hannah is praying with fervor and zeal, like someone I want to be when I pray. Hannah addresses God and His power. Hannah addresses God and His power! Hannah pours out herself and her heart to God—all while praying. This prayer will free so many hearts and souls.

Hannah speaks to the Lord, our Father, boldly and fervently. She proclaims while in prayer the miraculous sovereignty of God—a sovereignty that we ignore and neglect, or at least sacrifice.

Hannah teaches about God's will like most will never. This is not done often but Hannah does it well. She teaches about God's will and uses numerous examples of how God will have His own way, by His design and because He is Creator of all and Lord of all. As soon as we understand that better, we should be able to reach a better place for ourselves and a better relationship with God.

HANNAH'S VOICE

RECOGNIZE GOD'S WILL

If we do not understand anything else, we understand that Hannah can speak on following God's will. Likewise, we should understand that she can testify to waiting, patience, perseverance, integrity and respect. Lessons which we can all use some reinforcement.

Hannah points out that The Lord is single—handedly able to do all things. She starts with heaviest of topics.

Death. Birth. Poverty. Wealth. Infidelity. Betrayal. War. Civil unrest. Evil. Love. Fighting. Unforgiveness. Barren wombs. God does all of this on His time, according to the plans He has for those who are participants in His kingdom.

God's will requires you to recognize it. We need to recognize it so that we can align ourselves. God's will is difficult to honor. However, we need to honor it because we are a part of God's will. Honoring God's will means to avoid questioning God's will. Honoring God's will means that we seek our place within the boundaries of God's will so that we do our part to make God's will come alive. Honoring God's will means not questioning God about what He is doing or why He is doing it or how He will do it or when He will do it or finish doing it. God's will includes us and our needs and desires and our being. Who are we to question God's will when we are essentially questioning our very existence? While one may challenge that question, it stands to reason that if God wants the wind to blow today but not tomorrow, He can also so choose to stop my breath while starting someone else's. This all part of God's will—none of which is subject to our challenge or questioning.

Recognizing God's will includes submitting to God's will, regardless of what we prefer. God's will is above our thoughts and our comprehension. We do not know why He does what He does and we do not have the right to ask. We especially do not have the right to expect an answer. This is the hardest detail for many of us. We forget that we are His children and He does not owe us an explanation. Follow the directions given to you by God, Jesus Christ, and the Holy Spirit. To the final detail. Do not modify the directions in any way. WE should not change the pathway to God's will. As soon as you do something that was different than God designed, that means that God has to do something extra to accommodate for your unapproved intervention.

Recognizing God's will means ultimate obedience. Complete obedience. Unwavering disobedience.

Honoring God's will means that we seek our place within the boundaries of God's will. What do you want me to do God? Stop and listen to His instructions. Recognize His voice and His instructions.

Are you already using the gifts that you have to further God's kingdom? If not, why not? When will you start? Do you see God's will within your own life? Do you share God's work within your life with others? Where does God want you to be? What does God want you to do? We answer those questions based on what God wants, rather than what we are willing to do. Our battles and our trials and our victories are chosen for us. We need to see that God's hand is upon us and He is truly guiding us so that His will may be done.

Honoring God's will means not questioning God. We sometimes unintentionally question God, but the rest of these questions are intentional and that question is intentionally disrespectful. God does not owe us an explanation about His will and what He does and what He denies us from having. We need to remember that God has a plan and if we are in God's will, then we will submit to His will. This is the problem: we only want to follow God's will when it fits into our desires.

HANNAH'S VOICE

When we question God, we are showing that we do not have faith in God and His plan. When we are questioning God, we are positioning ourselves to disrespect God. We cannot keep doing that and think that God is okay with you talking to Him that way. The other thing to that it does is that it gives us a false sense of power. Questioning God is not prohibited when it benefits the relationship, meaning it brings you closer. Questions such as 'how can I please You, Lord?' 'How can I seek You more?' 'What should I do to get closer to You, Lord?' These are questions that God can hear, answer and understand. God does not owe us an answer.

When you are able, read Job to see how God responded to Job when asked it all. Job 38 starts God's answer to Job. God did answer Job, but I don't want God to answer me in that manner. God answered him for 129 verses. In these verses, God questions Job about all that God had done. Job's response is a mere six verses, apologetically and remorsefully. Lesson learned! All of us should consider this a lesson as a lesson learned. We should walk away understanding that we should be wise enough to stop doing the foolish activity which causes us to gain God's attention in the wrong manner.

At some point, Job recognized God's will so he stepped back into the place God assigned. Hannah helps us with how to recognize God's will and still appeal to God's heart, soul, and mind because she recognized God's will. She wanted a baby but she needed to submit to God's will so that her baby would be a prophet and messenger for the Lord.

LET GOD'S WILL BE DONE

One of the most miraculous part of these verses is that Hannah let God's will be done because she recognized God's will earlier. She is committed to doing

God's will. Her praise is showing God that she is not excluded from praise and worship to God. When she remembered her promise and kept her promise and fulfilled her promise to God. She followed God's will!

God used her to fulfill His will for Samuel who eventually was used to expose God's selected King.

Hannah was part—a Big part—of God's will. Hannah was chosen because she could be trusted. God has already tested her heart. God saw that she was praying unrelentingly. This was her mission. She took it seriously. She handled it well.

Part of letting God's will be done is cooperating. We have to accept whatever God gives us. Verse seven reads, "God sends poverty and wealth; He humbles and He exalts." For those who are labeled as poverty, they may be in poverty so that they put down pride and ask for and accept assistance. Poverty and pride need to divorce as partners, because so often they are. Poverty is solved with help and support. Wealth is designed to help and share. God can change those financial accoutrements at any time. God changes that situation based on what God needs to happen.

Remember we are part of a plan that we did not design and that we do not know the path and that we do not create the ending.

God designs who He humbles and who He exalts. Our job is to accept and carry out our role in God's will. It is also not our job to second guess God's plan and His methods and who He uses and especially do not question or second guess who God chooses to bless.

Don't interfere with God's work. We are always trying to 'help' God do what we think we thought He wanted. So we help and 'muddy up' the situation so that now God has to course correct or worse God has to change His plans because you decide to interfere or not cooperate.

HANNAH'S VOICE

Letting God's will be done may involve you not getting what you feel is fair. You may be held away from obvious blessings. You may be kept in a holding pattern until God's will is done.

I was in that space for six years, maybe actually seven, while I was waiting for God to do His work. The level of patience and perseverance required to survive God's timing and during His test of us is required.

I will be the first to testify that enduring and following God's will is hard but I don't have to be first. We have other examples of being aligned with God's will is how we share our love for Him and remember that God is in control.

God can see everything! God knows everything!

Let God's will be done. Allow God to show you that He loves you despite how you feel. I know that it's easy to say but I have been in that position and I am there often.

SUBMIT TO GOD'S WILL

Hannah has a tough situation—am I ever going to have a baby?! She pleads before the Lord. She asks Him graciously, yet boldly to give her a child. She was decent; she was orderly; she asked fervently. Her intentions were pure. She was taunted. Yet she submitted to God's will. She considered and pondered in her heart whether she would be content to be without children. Her husband said that he gives her more and more of himself because of it, but she was serious about a child.

POWERFUL LESSONS IN PRAYER

Then she made the ultimate ultimatum and sacrifice, she bargained with God that if God gave her a child, she would take that child to the church to be dedicated to God for all of his days.

I do not know whether it was initially God's will to give her Samuel but I believe God did give her Samuel because she demonstrated a resounding faith with an amazing attitude and flourishing spirit.

I really believe that she would have been content to resolve without children but look what an example she is because God did. Because she submitted to God, remained faithful to God, God was able to decide and discern the character of Hannah.

This all happened because she submitted to God's will. She was willing to submit to God's will.

We do not usually submit to God's will without coercion and coaxing. We do not understand how our misdirected behavior created issues for God's plan. Why can't we just follow God's will? Because we think we are knowledgeable about the plan. The problem with us is that we do not know the plan and we do not know what our plan interference costs us or others later.

Submission is not optional. I am not special! Why do I think that I can avoid God's will? I am not different from Moses, David, Hannah, Samuel, Ruth, Naomi, Mary or Jesus.

We cannot avoid God's will especially since Jesus still died when we would have quit. We cannot avoid God's will!

Consider all that has been God's will. Your birth. Your education. Your career. Your family. Your goals. Your creativity. Your thoughts. You. What if someone did not do their part to make God's will a reality for your life? What would you do if you found out that someone opted out of their responsibilities? But do you realize that even when I do not do what I am supposed to do, God can still fulfill His will. God uses whomever He wants to do His will.

Saul was not following God anymore so God chose David. David got beside himself, so God chose Solomon. God's will be done! God's will will be done!

Why is it so hard to submit to God's will? My guess that we are all narcissist—we need to think we are in control at some level. We start to submit by relinquishing control to God of our whole lives. It is also hard because we do not know the plan so we think we need our own plan. We do not have enough faith to allow God to do His Perfect Will without our interference. We feel like God needs help. Well, I have news for all of us: God does NOT need our help. He created the plan before us. He did NOT need our help then and He certainly does not need our help now.

When we 'help,' we need to be cautious that we are not giving others the impression that God is at work through our actions, actions which are not authorized by God.

Is God's will hard to understand? Yes.

Is God's will hard to believe? Yes.

Is God's will hard to accept? Yes.

Is God's will hard to submit to? Yes.

Is God's will hard to follow? Yes.

Is God's will hard to share? Yes.

Submit?

Submit.

Submit!

Hannah teaches submission is her prayer, in her attitude, in the actions, and in her perseverance. She speaks to the to the fact that God can reverse your situation like He did hers. God will erase your hardships based on His will. God will change your life and its situations and circumstances based on His perfect will. He gives His will based on what we will do based on the exercise of His will.

Recognize.

Let.

Submit.

Amen.

HANNAH'S VOICE

POWERFUL LESSONS IN PRAYER

Hannah Shares Valuable Insight

1 Samuel 2:9-11

⁹ He will guard the feet of his faithful servants,

   but the wicked will be silenced in the place of darkness.

"It is not by strength that one prevails;

¹⁰   those who oppose the Lord will be broken.

The Most High will thunder from heaven;

   the Lord will judge the ends of the earth.

"He will give strength to his king

   and exalt the horn of his anointed."

¹¹ Then Elkanah went home to Ramah, but the boy ministered before the Lord under Eli the priest.

SERMON

GOD PROTECTS

Hannah prays the promise that God will protect His faithful servants. How would she know that? Because He protected her. He protected her from her doubt, her fear, and the enemy. And herself. God guards against the misdirected and misguided where we may find ourselves. God guards us from our enemies and situations, dangerous and unwholesome. God guards us from sin that we are clearly trying to entertain.

God protects our minds when we doubt and fear. When we doubt ourselves. When we doubt God. Fear and doubt are horrible enemies that will eat away at the very fiber of your being. When we doubt and fear, we do not fulfill our purpose or our dreams or goals. With doubt and fear, we question God and the

HANNAH'S VOICE

Holy Spirit and God's will. Our faith will not exist in the same place as doubt and fear.

God protects our hearts: the heart that He created. God protects our hearts from all that happens. He does not allow us to be completely crushed. He does not allow everyone to see us, because God protects us. When God protects our hearts, He keeps us in close proximity to Him so that healing can take place quickly.

I have been in relationships where God told me to protect my heart and God did it for me. When the relationship ended, I was not the empty vessel that I could have been. I was not broken the way I was supposed to be. Instead, I reached for God and I confided in God and He nourished my spirit and comforted my soul.

God protects our bodies. This is a HUGE task. We subject our bodies to the worst. I live in the most obese city, Houston, Texas, according to a national study. I am overweight. I do not treat my body well at all. I am just too lazy to workout, but anxious to eat. Is that of God? Not at all.

God tries to protect us from others who intend to harm us. Do we assist our enemies? Are we in places we should not be? Doing what we should not be doing? With persons we should not be associating? If any of that is true, then we make it hard, nearly impossible, to allow God to protect us.

God's job, which He created, is to protect us, even from ourselves. This is a hard lesson and difficult to understand. We are our own worst enemy. We stand in our own way. We keep ourselves in trouble.

God protects our souls. When satan asked for Job, God consented to access of everything but Job's soul. God ultimately protects your soul. Your soul is where care, love, kindness, and concern live. Your soul is where your character originates. Your soul is a place conditioned and prepared for God—and only

God. Your soul is the part of you that cries out to God in surrender and reconciliation, in love and fear, in remorse and joy, in pain and supplication. Your soul belongs to God and no one else! Your soul requires protection! Anything that belongs to God is subject to attack! You and your soul are subject to be attacked! The devil asked for Job and Simon Peter. The devil asked for all of us. God has to permit us to be 'touched,' but He does not sacrifice our souls. If God won't sacrifice our soul, when why would we?

We sacrifice our souls when we do not read and study God's word, when we do not pray, when we do not love others, and when we avoid God.

Some of us have gifts and callings on our lives which we never answer. That is an insult to God. This is rejecting God.

Your soul is important. It is your connection to God and we put ourselves in jeopardy when we bargain our soul away for other people and activities and stuff. Stop selling your soul to the devil! Nothing is worth you owing your soul to the devil. Remember that your soul does not belong to you! You have NO authority to bargain or negotiate what belongs to God!

It is hard to protect what you cannot trust! God will guard the feet of His faithful servants—not the wandering, wavering, uncertain, indecisive, and easily persuaded.

GOD PREVAILS

Prevail is defined as "to be widespread or current; exist everywhere or generally" and "to be prove superior in strength, power, or influence."

HANNAH'S VOICE

God prevails! There are times when we think that WE prevailed, but actually it was God who prevailed. God won. God got the score. God got the victory. God outran the competition. God overwhelmed the other person. We cannot take credit for anything that happens. We cannot take credit for any of the results. God strengthens us for the fights we are in and situations we encountered and circumstances where we find ourselves surviving. It is God! It is God who prevails!

God prevails over His enemies and those outside of God's will. When God allows us to be victorious, that victory is a part of God's will; not an opportunity to gloat or brag. That not only deserves public praise to God, you owe God an apology for trying to take what does not belong to you.

God prevails. Because God prevails, we then can prevail. I am encouraged by that because God could separate me from His victory. God could neglect to allow me to share in His victory while I do not deserve it while believing that I do; but clearly I do not.

The scripture reads: 'those who oppose the Lord will be broken.' With that in mind, I do not willfully oppose God. You see I do not need to live in a manner that I disrespect God, dismantle God's plans, disregard God's directions and God's orders for my steps, or dismiss the importance of the voice of the Holy Spirit. These are behaviors we exercise everyday. We disrespect, dismantle, dismiss, and disregard God daily. We do it defiantly or systematically or unconsciously, but we ALL do it. Just in case we do not know the word for it, it is sin. These actions actually constitute sin. Sin is an opposition of God. We should be silenced and broken for what we do to God. We should be silenced and broken for sabotaging God's plans, especially when we are otherwise unaware of our actions. We can never claim that we do not have that effect on the steps of God's plans.

The good thing is that God forgives us. God offers us His peace. God does this in spite of what we do and do not do. God prevails when He forgives us as well. God forgives us when we cannot forgive ourselves.; God forgives us when we do not forgive others, even though God said He would not.

God prevails.

God strengthens.

GOD PROVIDES

God provides. God provides. God provides. Only God provides. The gravity of that statement is sobering and humbling and staggering. If you start to make a list of what God provides, what would you list? Here is my initial list:

Breath

Life

Sight

Hearing

Taste

Intellect/smarts

Touch

Blood

Veins

HANNAH'S VOICE

Smell

The Bible

The Holy Spirit

Jesus Christ

Love

Forgiveness

Arms

Legs

Lungs

What would you add to the list? Whatever you added to the list is certainly what God provides. The most important part to understand is that God provides EVERYTHING!

Often, that is the first thing we forgot: that we do NOT provide anything. God provides. So that we can have what we need to do His will and glorify Him.

One such provision is strength. Strength is required to follow God. To be a disciple of God and Jesus Christ, there is a cost. For that cost, we need strength and several other elements.

How does God provide strength? God gives us the ability to stand on His word when trouble comes. Lack of strength means that we seek our go-to's which is nearly void of God. If Hannah had not been given God's strength, then Hannah may have cursed at Peninnah and would have disappointed God. If Hannah did not have God's assigned strength, then Hannah may have quit praying and stopped believing in God and God's provision. You know how we can be: one issue can cause us to question God and ALL that He has ever done; causing our selective memory to kick-in. We start to forget that God has saved us from so much and kept us sheltered from harm. We can be sure that God's plan is the best timing for us. The scripture reads, which Hannah does not have the benefit of, "all things work together for the good of those who love God and are called according to His purpose." Romans 8:28.

God provides a way out of sin. God provides a way toward success. God provides peace—a peace which transcends our understanding, Philippians 4:7. God provides strength through peace and love. God's peace is so supernatural that we do not understand it, we cannot explain it and others cannot appreciate it.

God's peace is like a breeze when the heat is about to consume you. God's peace keeps you calm and sane. God's peace reminds you that God is with you and He will not forsake you. God's peace increases your self-esteem and self-worth. God's peace covers all issues and solves all of the problems that most of us deal with: anger. God's peace keeps anger at bay. God's peace keeps you close to Him. God's peace can overcome your biggest issues and your strongest fears.

God's love is a provision of strength. Love covers a multitude of sins, 1 Peter 4:8. God provides me with a love which covered all of my sins: Jesus Christ. Jesus' strength was God's provision. God's strength birthed Jesus. God's strength taught Jesus. God's strength led Jesus to the temples to educate others. God strengthened Jesus to lead thousands to God. God gave the strength that Jesus needed to be accused, be persecuted, be flogged, be lied on, be abused, to walk His own cross up a hill, and be nailed to a cross to die so that we could live. God gave Jesus strength to stay on that cross and not come down. God's strength overrides your fear. God's strength overcomes your doubt. I can only imagine how Hannah felt when she realized what God had done after all of her prayers—planted a baby within her body. This is an exhibit of peace and love and resolve.

God provides love. In 1 Corinthians 13, God defines love using Paul's pen. In John, God defines love using Jesus' life. In Matthew, God defines love using Mary and Elizabeth's bodies.

God provides love so that we can love others. God replenishes that love, so that we never run out. God provides lessons on how to love, so we can love the people we will encounter. We do not love others because of two reasons: 1) we do not love ourselves; and, 2) we think we are the replenisher of our love. We are NOT the replenishers of our own love tanks. God is. God replenishes our love tanks and the ability to love others. God provides strength to overcome our self-hatred so that you can love yourself, and so that you can love others.

God provides you to love others. God provides others to love you.

God provides.

GOD'S PLACEMENT FOR PRO RE NATA

Pro Re Nata means 'for an unforeseen need or contingency.' God created pro re nata. God is for unforeseen needs or/and contingencies. Everything that happens is unforeseen to us; but not to God. God sees everyone. God overcomes all of that based on His will. Most of us panic at this thought: we cannot rely on our own plans for situations, struggles and stress. God has the Big Glasses on so He knows how the best solution affects the next steps and the next part of your life.

POWERFUL LESSONS IN PRAYER

God also possesses the contingency plan for all that happens and whatever does not happen. God has THE PLAN; not a plan.

Let's recall a few examples of the plan for the unforeseen. The first solution for our sin was the flood. God choose Noah to stay. The second solution for our sin was multiple famines—not as severe as the floods, but severe all the same. The third solution for our sins was the death, burial, and resurrection of Jesus Christ. WE cannot continue to behave in a manner which causes God to fix our mess. We keep thinking that we are in charge, yet we are not.

God's placement is effective because God knows it all. Let's examine willful disobedience while falling out of favor with God. Saul was removed as king. Do you think that if Saul had quit acting disrespectfully that he would have been replaced? I don't think so. I believe had Saul behaved better, then he would have still been king, but because God knew Saul's tendencies then God already selected Saul's replacement, David. God keeps us all in our roles and positions so that God's will can be done.

My daughter plays basketball. When the post player is out of position then the point guard cannot execute the play called by the coach. So when the Coach, God, designs a plan, God, the Coach, shares that plan with Jesus, the point guard, and the Holy Spirit, the center. We are guards in this life. That guard position means that we shoot when the ball is given to us. It could also mean we pass the ball back to Jesus Christ, the point guard to reset the play. It means taking a time—out to consult with God about how the play should be run. This may seem like an unrelated example however, we have to consider that we are in a grander plan, a larger discipline, so that means that we need to be sure that we do our part. When all of the players do not do their individual part on the basketball court, then the team loses.

HANNAH'S VOICE

Do we really want to be substituted by someone else because we could not do the job to fulfill the will of God? I do not want to be substituted. When I think about David missing the opportunity to build a temple because of something he did, I do not want that to be my story. Solomon built the temple. I hope that I have not already been substituted in areas of life where I most desire.

God has a plan for the hiccups we make in life. We are in our own way 90% of the time. We do not realize that we are our own worst enemy in regards to progress we need to make. Let's examine some examples. One of my favorite characters of the Bible is Joseph. His story is one of mischief of others rather than himself. Joseph's brothers envied him so much that they tried to kill him. He then was sold into a foreign land so that he could save them later. The brothers would have sabotaged themselves and their lives, except God had the real plan that we view as a contingency plan. WE are ever grateful that God's plan was in effect. We will always do what we want and then go back and ask God to 'bless' our actions, attitudes, and behaviors. Then when we really mess it up, we plead with God to correct our mess and correct it in our favor; not to mention right now.

What else could Joseph's brothers say when he made himself known to them? They did not know the Lord as their Father like Joseph did. They had to lie to get the stage set for forgiveness, which God had already prepared in advance. Genesis 50:20 reads, "You intended to harm me, but God intended it for good to accomplish what is now being done, the saving of many lives."

Joseph could say that because he was walking in his purpose. Hannah walked into her purpose. Ruth walked into her purpose. David walked to into his purpose. Jesus walked in His purpose. So did the Holy Spirit.

Although some of us are still investigating our purpose, we now know that God has purposed us for His plans and if we are obedient to God and delight about

His will, we too will walk into and function within our purpose. God has a plan and His entire plan accommodates our decisions and mistakes and missteps.

Hannah shares these points with us which is valuable insight. God protects. God prevails. God provides. God places. We each experience these actions in our lives; we simply need to be sensitive to recognize when God is moving around and moving us around as it relates to His will and how we are to serve others.

Amen.

HANNAH'S VOICE

Acknowledgements

God, thank You for Your plans for me. Thank You for **Hannah's Voice: Powerful Lessons in Prayer,** and choosing me to complete Your project. I just want to please You, God. Thank You for continuing to anoint me and to invest in me and my gifts, which keep surprising me. Thank You for loving and forgiving me.

Hillary and Nehemiah, thank you for supporting me and my endeavors. Thank you for loving me, especially when I do nothing without a pen and a clipboard, thank you for enduring my late nights, your ideas, the sounding board, the love and the support. Thank you for celebrating our legacy.

Kimberly Joiner, thank you for reading my work and offering your feedback. Your contribution is invaluable.

To my prayer partners and to my accountability partners, thank you for the long talks and the powerful prayers and the encouragement.

To the readers who this will reach and empower and touch and affect, may these words empower you and help you reach some resolve. May you be inspired to achieve your goals and dreams. May you enhance your relationship with God so that your other relationships will also improve. May you enhance your self-esteem through prayer and study. May you have courage and peace. Share love the best you can until you can share love without reservation.

HANNAH'S VOICE

Minister Onedia N. Gage seeks to share her outlandish pursuit of God with her prayers, study and meditation. She desires to share her faith in a manner which helps you do the same through her calling. She hopes that these words bless you.

Please feel free to contact and share your testimony. onediagage@onediagage.com, or @onediangage (twitter). www.onediagage.com

Blogtalkradio.com/onediagage

Youtube.com/onediagage

Facebook.com/onedia-gage-ministries

HANNAH'S VOICE

POWERFUL LESSONS IN PRAYER

PREACHER ♦ PRAYER WARRIOR ♦ TEACHER

To invite Rev. Gage to preach, teach, and pray, Please contact us at

@onediangage (twitter) ♦ onediagage@onediagage.com ♦ facebook.com/onediagage

youtube.com/onediagage ♦ blogtalkradio.com/onediagage ♦ www.onediagage.com

HANNAH'S VOICE

Publishing

Do you have a book you want to write, but do not know what to do?

Do you have a book you need to publish but do not know how to start?

Would publishing move your career forward?

Let us help

onediagage@purpleink.net ♦ www.purpleink.net

713.705.5530 ♦ 281.740.5143